CHILTON, WINDLESTONE AND RUSHYFORD

An Industrial and Social History

by
Brian Turner

Published by Brian Turner in 1999
New South View, Chilton, Ferryhill, Co. Durham, DL17 0PS

Printed and bound in Great Britain by J. Snowball & Son, Dundas Street, Spennymoor, Co. Durham.

To

Audrey,

for her support and

encouragement,

and

to our dear nephew, Peter.

Introduction

Chilton is an industrially developed village that owes its earlier existence to the presence of coal seams, which lie at some depth beneath its surface. For many years the village was divided into three areas: Dene Bridge, Chilton Buildings and Windlestone. The major expansion in the early part of the twentieth century was due entirely to the success of Chilton and Windlestone Collieries.

A shaft had been sunk as early as 1833 at Dene Bridge, but it was not until the 1870s that the small hamlet of Chilton Buildings progressed with the repairing of the shaft at Dene Bridge and the sinking of a new one, followed a few years later by the sinking of shafts at Windlestone, its site now occupied by Chilton Junior School. This brought about the building of Dene Bridge and Windlestone Rows, to house the miners at both pits. As time went by, expansion brought the two communities together, forming the Chilton that we know today.

The miners' houses are still there; many are privately owned and, with the passing of time, a number of housing estates have sprung up, making an attractive contribution to the village.

Rushyford is less than half a mile to the south of the village and has always been associated with Chilton. It is located on the former Windlestone Estate once owned by the powerful Eden family.

I have many pleasant memories of growing up in Chilton and Windlestone, playing on the old pitheaps of disused Windlestone Colliery and watching the steam locomotives going over Chilton level crossing with trucks brimful of coal. There were groups of pitmen on their way home after a shift at the pit, walking from Dene Bridge Row, on through the village, some as far as Prospect Terrace over a mile away, their faces as black as the coal seams they were working in, striding out with their hobnailed boots rattling on the pavements. These and many other memories are stamped indelibly on my mind, for life.

My interest in times past was brought about by a chance conversation with a man named Tommy Buckle, an old resident of the village. I had known him since I was a boy. His hobby of writing down events in the village as they happened and collecting anything of interest was something he thought no one else cared about. He met with no one who shared these interests. However, I was interested and told him so. "I will ask my wife, Ada, to let you have anything of interest relating to Chilton and Windlestone, should anything happen to me," he replied.

With Tom's passing, his memorabilia came to me and, along with some of my own, I endeavoured to put it into some sort of order. From these beginnings I have written the following pages. It is not intended to be a precise history of the two communities and, whilst most of it is correct, I make my apology now for any inaccuracies one might uncover.

The progress and expansion of our two communities was, for many years, tied to the success or failure of our two coal mines.

The reader will find many references to mining in this book which I hope are simplified enough for their understanding. For the most part I have enjoyed the learning process of putting all the bits and pieces together and meeting the many people who have helped me along the way to complete this tale.

My purpose is to pass on to the community an opportunity to see how it was for our predecessors and how the heritage of the village has evolved over the last 200 years.

Brian Turner, 1999.

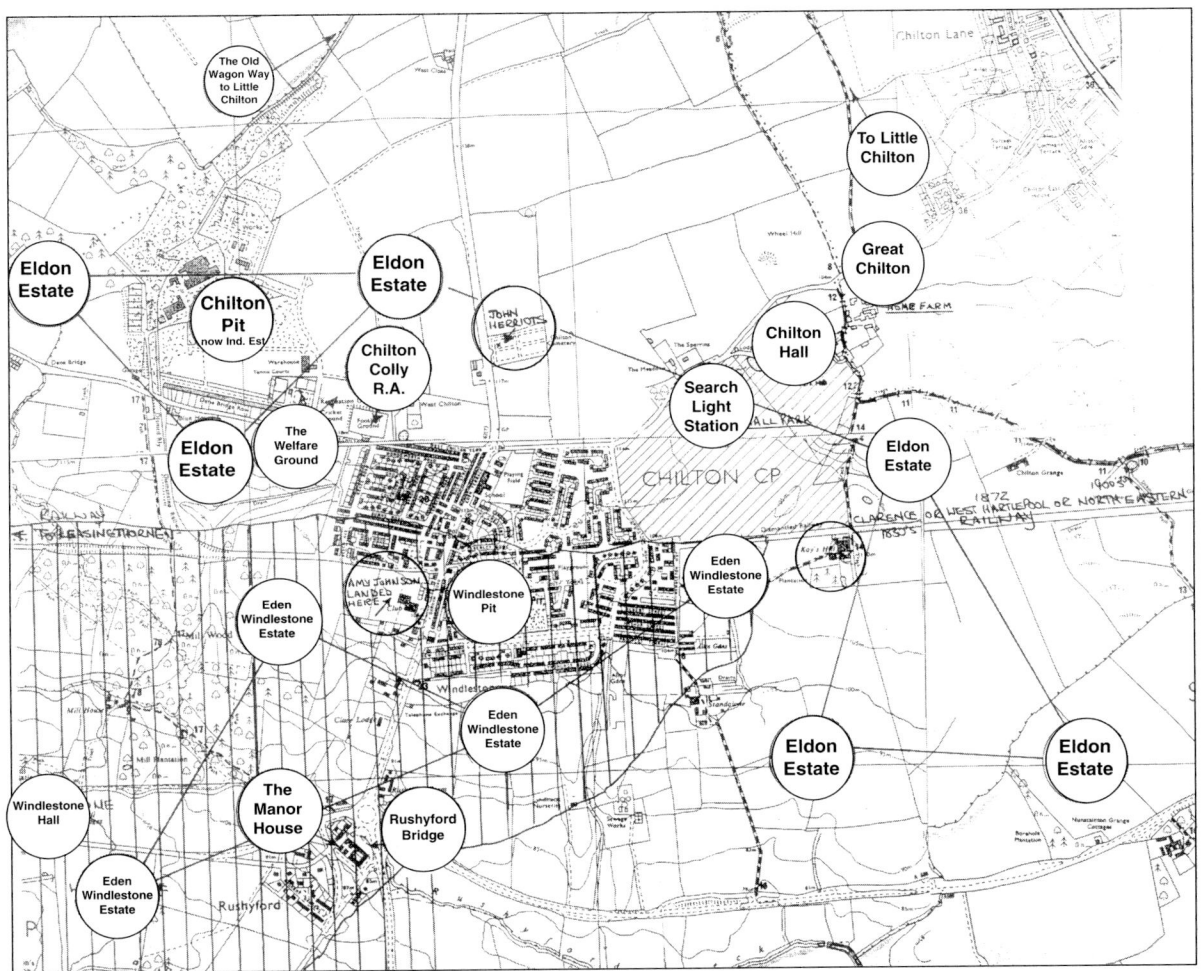

Location of the Eden/Eldon Estates in Chilton and Windlestone incorporating various sites relevant throughout the book

Contents

CHAPTER ONE

No Time like the Present

No Time like the Present

Chilton in 1999 has come a long way since its humble beginnings, when the coal underneath its surface brought about a growth and expansion starting back in the 1870s which still goes on today in many ways, despite the demise of the pits - and all under one banner we call progress.

Improvements in housing, modern conveniences, education and leisure, along with a much improved environment, have given the resident a standard of living and comfort which generations gone by could only have dreamed of.

There is no time like the present: the organisations and groups who provide services to the community and do their best to improve our quality of life appears to be as good a place as any for our tale to start. Follow this with a journey back into the past to see how our forebears fared in creating our heritage and, later on, continue with the present as we approach the millennium.

Chilton Parish Council.

In the 1800s Chilton, as part of the Ferryhill Parish, had little or no say in its own affairs. By the l900s, our two collieries were responsible for a massive expansion in housing and population, bringing with it a stronger voice resulting in the people of Chilton and Windlestone being able to elect councillors to represent them, giving authority to local people and allowing them to discuss and decide their own affairs.

Chilton Parish Council Offices, Hutton House, an imposing detached house facing onto the main road in the centre of the village 1999

*Chilton Junior School 1999
Designated to become a primary
school in the year 2002*

From the humble beginnings of almost a century ago there have been many who have given their time and effort to the welfare of our community. It continues with our present councillors upholding the traditions and principles of the past, looking forward and endeavouring to improve the conditions and amenities of the village.

Chilton Parish Councillors assembled for one of their monthly meetings October 1999
back row l - r: *George Elliott, Brian Turner, Jenny Ratcliffe, Maureen Errington, Glenda Attwood, Lily Dixon, Alan Bruce* **front row l - r:** *Patrick McCourt, Alan Grey (Clerk), Lenny Potts (Chairman), Barry Jones (Vice-Chairman), Joe Lee, Victor Collison*

Schools

Chilton Junior School and Community College

The school has shared its site and some of its facilities with the village Community Association since 1983, having been built originally as a secondary school in 1963 before becoming a junior school in 1973. The joint use of the school has great advantages for both partners: the school has immediate community involvement and a major source of income, whilst the active Community College, as it is known, has use of the excellent facilities. Accommodation is provided on three floors with extensive outdoor amenities.

On the ground floor there are seven spacious classrooms, one of which has a kiln. The administration of the school is on this level, along with the main hall, gym, dining hall and community facilities, including a squash court. The school fields are in use for the children, and are also used by a number of village football teams. The Social Club housed within the complex has been running successfully for a number of years, adding to the all-year-round amenities.

Chilton Infant and Nursery School

Formerly Chilton Council School, it has provided education for countless girls and boys for the last 90 years. Sadly, this proud old school will see the last of its children move on to our new primary school (now the junior school) after extensive alterations are completed by 2002.

Chilton Branch Library.

This library, opened in 1974, has recently celebrated its 25th birthday. It is a meeting place for the regular user and has been the focal point of many exhibitions and fun evenings. The librarian, Sue Bolam, and her staff, can take credit for much of the hard work involved. It retains an intimate atmosphere and will soon be involved in a millennium exhibition charting the progress of the village.

A nostalgic scene with the afternoon sun bringing out the different shapes and design of Chilton Infant and Nursery School

Chilton Branch of Durham County Library 1999.

With an eye to the future as well as the past, a new function of the library will be to house a permanent display of artifacts depicting the heritage of the village and will, in effect, become our new Heritage Centre.

Chilton Health Centre

This building was formerly a First Aid dressing station and, through the 1939-45 war was used by the Air Raid Precautions Unit (ARP) and Civil Defence. Doctors used to have their own surgeries adjoining the house: Kilkee House, adjacent to Westwood Terrace; Hutton House, now used by the Parish Council; and Clare Lodge, were three of them. The amalgamation of doctors to form a Health Centre in Chilton occurred about 1966.

The former Dressing Station is extended to the rear to form Chilton Health Centre

What's in a Name?

Chilton

A common name, usually, one interpretation Child-Tun meaning the Children's Tun, but it is unlikely that this can always be the exact meaning.

Cild was used as a title for a youth of noble birth, a Prince of the Royal Blood.

There are several other names beginning with Chil. With regard to the second half of the name, Tun, this originally meant a fence or enclosure, but at an early age developed the meaning, enclosure round a house, village or town.

There are many variations of the word Chilton throughout history. Some of them are as follows:

Childatun - 565 AD, Cyldatuun - 891, Ciltona - 1091, Chiltune 1180, and Magna Chiltona 1214. The name Chilton, however, has been around a long time, as far back as 1254 and probably even earlier.

Windlestone

Derived from Wildlesden about 1106. In the 13th century, Wynelisdon meant Winels Hill. Windliston has its origin probably from the Roman and meaning a settlement of soldiers. In 1448, Cecilia, wife of John Windliston deceased, confirmed to John Wyndliston, her son and heir, his half heritage: 2 *messuages, 5 oxgangs and 12 acres of land and 3 of meadow, in the village of Wyndlistone.

Here, the family name has changed in one generation; the village, presumably, is in the area of the Edens' Windlestone estate. There are various changes through the ages: Windlesden, Winelsdon, Wydellesdown and Wyndellesdon, to name but a few.

There were a number of families settled in the Windlestone area, all landowners. One example in 1521, was that of Thomas Marton, Gentleman, of Marton in Craven. He gave to William Wren of Shirburn, County Durham, to Richard Pkynson of Beamond Hill, and, to William Raket of Durham, 1 messuage and 50 acres of land and 2 of meadow in Wyndliston, formally held by Robert Denton.

There are many instances of transactions and as many different names. By 1635, the name Windlestone appears. At that time, land at Windlestone, once the property of Nesham Convent, was purchased by the Crown after the dissolution of the monasteries. It was then conveyed by Robert Steavenson to Robert Eden Esq. of Windlestone.

*Messuage: a dwelling house with buildings or land about it.

CHAPTER TWO

The Edens of Windlestone

The Edens of Windlestone

Robert Johnson Eden,
5th Baronet

Sir William Eden, 7th Baronet

Sir Timothy Calvert Eden, 8th
Baronet

Robert Anthony Eden,
Earl of Avon KG, PC, MC, MP
Prime Minister

The Edens of Windlestone

The Edens were one of County Durham's most famous families, probably originating from the hamlet of Little Eden, in the Parish of Castle Eden. The old form of the name being de Eden, an ancestor of the present family was Robert de Eden, in the reign of Edward III 1327-77.

His marriage to the heiress of Ranulph de Preston brought the estate of Preston-on-Tees into the family, where it remained for 440 years. Through the centuries, the Edens made a number of important and influential matches. For example, in 1547 John Eden married Eliz, daughter and co-heir of William Lambton, bringing with her the estate of Bellasis in the parish of Billingham.

Previously, in 1538, John's father, William Eden, a Durham mercer, had left him considerable wealth, including land at Windlestone conveyed to him in trust. John's son, Robert Eden, married the daughter and co-heir of John Hutton of Hunwick in 1568, who brought the West Auckland estate into the Eden family.

Robert took part in the rising of 1569 and was arrested and carried off to Carlisle to await trial. He was imprisoned for some time before Lord Scroop had him transferred to Durham. He was set free on his bond being given, for his good behaviour. He and his wife lived in the Manor House at West Auckland, which came with his wife. Robert died in 1584, to be succeeded by his son, John.

In 1675, a Robert Eden, barrister, succeeded his father Colonel John Eden and married Margaret Lambton. They had 15 children. In 1672, Robert had been made Baronet of West Auckland and represented County Durham in seven Parliaments. Successive Edens made their mark as Members of Parliament, one becoming Mayor of Hartlepool.

The 3rd Baronet, Sir Robert, succeeded his father at the age of nine and, in 1739, married Mary Davidson of Beamish Park. This generation of Edens appears to have done well, with titles conferred on three sons of this family.

Robert, the second son, married Miss Calvert, sister of Lord Baltimore, who, as Lord Proprietary of the Province of Maryland, USA nominated Captain Eden as Governor in 1769. When the War of Independence began in 1776, General Lee gave orders for Governor Eden's arrest. The order was never carried out; consequently the Governor and his family were able to get away on HMS Foway to England.

Within a week of returning to London in the September, Robert Eden was created Baronet of Maryland. After the war he returned to Maryland to obtain restitution for his confiscated property, but unfortunately died from a fever shortly after his arrival.

William, the third son, was created Baron Auckland in 1793 after a long and distinguished career as a diplomat.

Morton, the eighth son, became an Ambassador, and also Lord Henly in the Irish peerage.

Windlestone Hall, now a residential school.

Robert Johnson Eden, 5th Baronet

He succeeded the title in 1812 at the age of 38 and inherited estates in Yorkshire from his grandmother. Unlike many of his forebears, he took little part in public affairs. Robert Johnson Eden sold the Preston-of-Tees estate and had the old house on the Windlestone estate pulled down to be replaced by a palatial hall at enormous cost.

Built about 1840 by Bonomi, one of the foremost architects of the day, the hall also included spacious estate offices, the whole of which was reputed to have cost £40,000. Robert designed the gardens surrounding the new hall; a host of new trees and shrubs were planted, adding to the natural beauty of the rolling landscape to the east and south, and enhancing an already attractive outlook.

By successive purchases through the centuries, the Edens had acquired possession of the whole township of Coundon, which also included Windlestone.

Sir William Eden, the 7th Baronet, controlled this area until his death in 1915. It was mainly during his lifetime and that of his family that the industrial history of Chilton and Windlestone developed.

The Windlestone estate was seven miles at its widest and covered 4,000 acres, taking in twenty farms as far away as Carrsides and most of the land where the town of Newton Aycliffe now stands. The estate continued to Rushyford, Chilton and westerly, taking in Leasingthorne, Coundon and Coundon Gate before sweeping back south-east to Middridge.

Lady Sybil Eden in her early twenties. A portrait by Sir Hubert von Herkomer.

The Eden family at Windlestone on the occasion of Sir William and Lady Sybil's Silver Wedding and John, the eldest son's coming of age. **l-r:**- *Timothy, Marjorie, Lady Sybil, Nicholas, Sir William, Anthony and John, behind Nicholas.*

Sir William Eden, 7th Baronet

Sir William Eden married the very beautiful Sybil Grey, who was born in India, daughter of Sir William Grey, the Governor of Bengal. Devoted parents, they had one daughter, Marjorie, the eldest, and four sons, John, Timothy, Anthony and Nicholas.

They lived in the manner befitting landed gentry, amidst magnificent gardens and parkland for which Sir William had a great passion. He was devoted to the care of his home, was a gifted watercolour artist and possessed a wonderful collection of paintings. He played a major role in the management of his large estate and, although he had a good income from the estate, he liked to spend it.

It is arguable as to whether or not the family motto applied to Sir William:

"Nallum numen abest si sit prudentia"

(Heaven will favour us, provided we are prudent)

The rent from the tenant farmers, although considerable, was added to immensely when leases were granted to Bolkow & Vaughan to work the coal beneath his land at Leasingthorne and

Anthony at 15

Middridge, and to Joseph Pease and Partners at Windlestone.

Pease's lease was for 63 years at £4,000 per annum, plus one shilling for every ton of coal brought to the surface. Pease also agreed to supply Sir William with 300 tons of best round coal each year, all this based on the mine working and not being stood down.

The smooth running of the estate depended to a large extent on the many workers employed in all kinds of skills and trades. They, in turn, relied on the Edens for their living, with expectations for their descendants to follow them on in the same employ. The Eden family had been on the site for almost four centuries, therefore no one would have cause to think it could be otherwise.

Sir William ensured his workers were well housed and paid a decent wage; at the same time, Lady Sybil made sure they were looked after if they were sick or in trouble. It appears that the Edens were good to their employees and were well served in return. No one could foresee, in the summer of 1911, the disaster to come with World War I or the breaking up of the estate in the great sale of 1936.

Lady Sybil never tired of involvement with the sick and injured. The nearest hospitals were at Durham and Darlington, 18 miles apart, with the South West Durham Coalfield in between. Lady Sybil's efforts, with the support of local groups, went a long way towards raising the funds necessary for a hospital to be built. A site was cleared at Bishop Auckland, the hospital was completed and named the Lady Eden Hospital. It still stands to this day, used as a day care centre.

With the onset of World War I, in 1914 the sad news was received that John had been killed at Ypres, Belgium. This was followed by the death Sir William in 1915.

By 1916, Windlestone Hall had been converted to a hospital for the Armed Forces and in the same year, Nicholas Eden, the youngest son at 16, joined the Navy after training at Dartmouth Naval College. He was killed at the Battle of Jutland in the same year.

War, unfortunately for all, is a great leveller. It will take the rich and the poor, the hard workers and the layabouts, and throw them all into the same melting pot. People go missing, lives are lost, and there are no real winners when one counts the cost. So it was for the Eden family: no different from any other, they had to count the cost, then get on with it and do the best they could for King and Country, just the same as everyone else.

Sir Timothy Calvert Eden, 8th Baronet

On the death of Sir William, and with John killed in action, Timothy succeeded to the title as the 8th Baronet. Incidentally, the title was only one of six double baronetcies in existence, the first being conferred on an ancestor in 1672 and on another member of the family in 1776.

In 1914, before the war had started, his intention was to go into the Diplomatic Service. With this in mind, Timothy went to Germany to learn the language. Meanwhile, relationships between England and Germany were deteriorating and future hostilities seemed to be imminent. Alas, Timothy left it too late to return home, and he was interned for an indefinite period.

In 1936, Sir Timothy sold the Windlestone Estate and moved south. He and his family lived in Fritham House, Lyndhurst in Hampshire, one of the highest locations in the New Forest. He served as a Staff Captain at the War Office in World War II and never ventured into politics. His main occupation was that of author, and he had several of his books published.

Sir Timothy Eden died in May 1963 aged 70, and was succeeded by his son John Eden MP.

Robert Anthony Eden

Robert Anthony Eden, Earl of Avon, KG, PC, MC Member of Parliment and Prime Minister.

Born in 1897, Robert Anthony. Son of William and Frances Sybil Eden. Abode, Windlestone. Quality, trade or profession of Father: Baronet. Taken from the baptismal records of the parish of Coundon.

At Aldershot aged 18

From the heading, one is aware that here was a boy destined to become the most famous Eden from a long line of distinguished ancestors.

His primary education, until he was nine years of age was undertaken at Windlestone with a governess. He spent a further five years at a preparatory school and, as befitted the son of an old, established family of landed gentry, he entered Eton College in 1911.

The First World War was the reason for young Anthony breaking his studies: he was keen to enlist into the army. He received his first commission at 19, the youngest of the company's subalterns by several years and the youngest in the British Army in 1916. He served with distinction in Belgium, saving a sergeant's life. His courageous conduct in the front line in France brought promotion and he was awarded the Military Cross. By the end of the First World War he was the youngest Brigade Major in the British Army at the age of 20.

Eden returned home to complete his education at Oxford and, for a while, considered entering the Diplomatic Service, before deciding to go into politics. In 1923, he won the seat at Warwick and Leamington for the Conservative Party when he was only 26, a seat he retained for the next 34 years. Handsome, over six feet tall and highly decorated in World War 1, Eden married Beatrice Helen Beckett in the same year as his first election victory. She complained that her honeymoon had been reduced to two days because of the General Election campaign.

In 1926, Eden, still in his twenties, was appointed Parliamentary Private Secretary to Chamberlain, the Foreign Secretary.

By the mid-30s, he was a member of the Cabinet. At 38, he was appointed Foreign Secretary, occupying the second most senior position after the Prime Minister.

Unrest in Europe, leading up to the Second World War in 1939, had Eden and many of his colleagues believing that compromise and some concessions might serve to satisfy Germany and so avoid a war. Churchill, on the other hand, did not think it would work. As it happened he was right, and was dismayed to see Eden eventually split with Chamberlain and resign as Foreign Secretary.

Anthony Eden

After the outbreak of war, Eden returned to government as Secretary for War. Shortly after this, he was back once more as Foreign Secretary in 1940 and stayed there until the war was over in 1945. In the same year, Eden found himself on the opposition bench in the role of deputy leader, after Labour's landslide victory. He played a major part in modernising the Conservative Party, with them returning to power, under Churchill in the 1951 elections. Eden returned to his old job as Foreign Secretary and, at 54, was at his peak. Popular both at home

and abroad, his standing in the government continued to grow.

In l953, Churchill suffered a stroke. Two years later, with Eden his chosen successor, he retired and Eden became Prime Minister. Less than two years later, Eden himself was in poor health and was forced to take an immediate rest. On his return, he found he was no longer able to carry on, and he resigned on January 9th 1957, to be succeeded by Harold Macmillan.

As Foreign Secretary, Eden would have few equals. A born diplomat, his workrate was phenomenal. He was a gentleman, in the true sense of the word, and highly respected among his contemporaries. In his retirement, Eden lived a quiet life with his second wife, Clarissa Spencer Churchill, a niece of Sir Winston, at his home the, Manor House, Alvediston in Wiltshire. He wrote a number of books and devoted much of his time to his memoirs, which covered a long and distinguished political career.

In 1961, he received a peerage and was given the title, Earl of Avon. Eden was a man of outstanding ability; for decades he graced the political scene and, more than most, left his mark on British foreign affairs.

Anthony Eden, born at Windlestone, spent his boyhood growing up among the parks and woodlands of his father's estate at the turn of the nineteenth century. As a young man he survived the horrors of the First World War and succeeded to the highest public office in the land.

In one of his books, "Another World 1897-1917", Eden remembers "as a very young child, being met by carriage at Bradbury Station with its wooden building and benevolent stationmaster, where the express train from the South was stopped for us. By the time I was a schoolboy, the hay store at Windlestone had been converted into garages for my father's motor cars, and we would then be driven the ten miles to Darlington station where we boarded the southbound express, but further up the line to London".

Robert Anthony Eden: Earl of Avon, KG, PC, MC died at his home in January 1977 and is buried in the village churchyard at Alvediston. A man of integrity and unquestionable ability, we can claim him as our most famous son from Windlestone.

Left: The Chapel on the estate at Windlestone.

CHAPTER THREE

Windlestone Colliery and Village

Windlestone Colliery and Village

Geology in the Chilton Area

Geology is a science related to the different layers of rock (strata) which form the earth's crust. It is fundamental to the industrial beginnings of Chilton, where coal seams are present in the strata at various depths from the surface. All of this brought about by the forces of nature over many millions of years.

The pattern of rock formation undergoes many changes on its way from the Pennines in the west to the north-east coast. An example of how it affects Chilton and Windlestone is shown in the section of strata shown on pages 30 and 31.

The geology of the county, from west to east, consists of a succession of rock layers, Carboniferous, Permian and Triassic, which all dip gently to the east. The Pennines is an anticlinal ridge raised up in the late Palaeozoic era. The Pennines were originally composed of three principal strata of rock, the topmost of these being the Coal Measures, which were separated from the lowest stratum, the Carboniferous Limestone, by a band of Millstone Grit. Extensive erosion and weathering have worn away the two upper layers of rock, thus exposing the Carboniferous Limestone in a number of places. The Millstone Grit, however, still forms the cap of the fell tops and ridges running to the east. The Pennines are, therefore, flanked on either side by the Millstone Grit and the Coal Measures.

A section through the Pennines

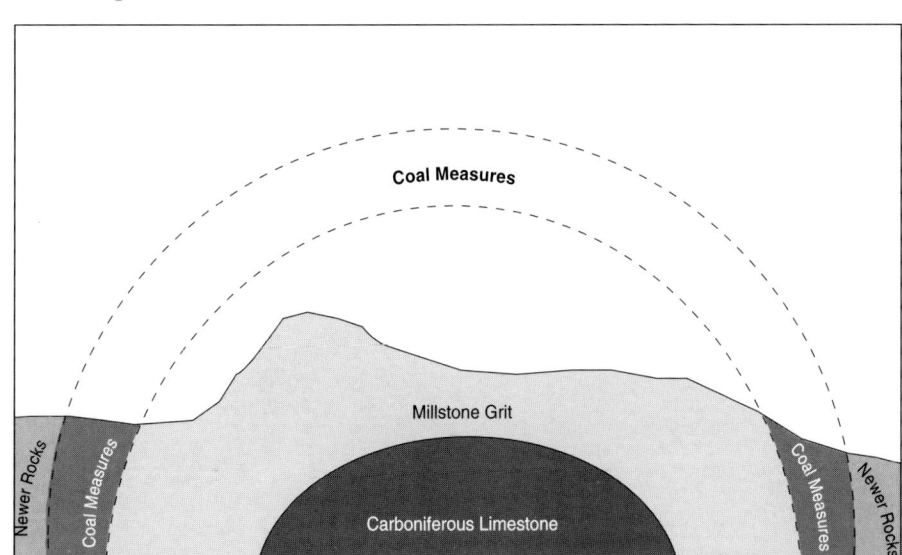

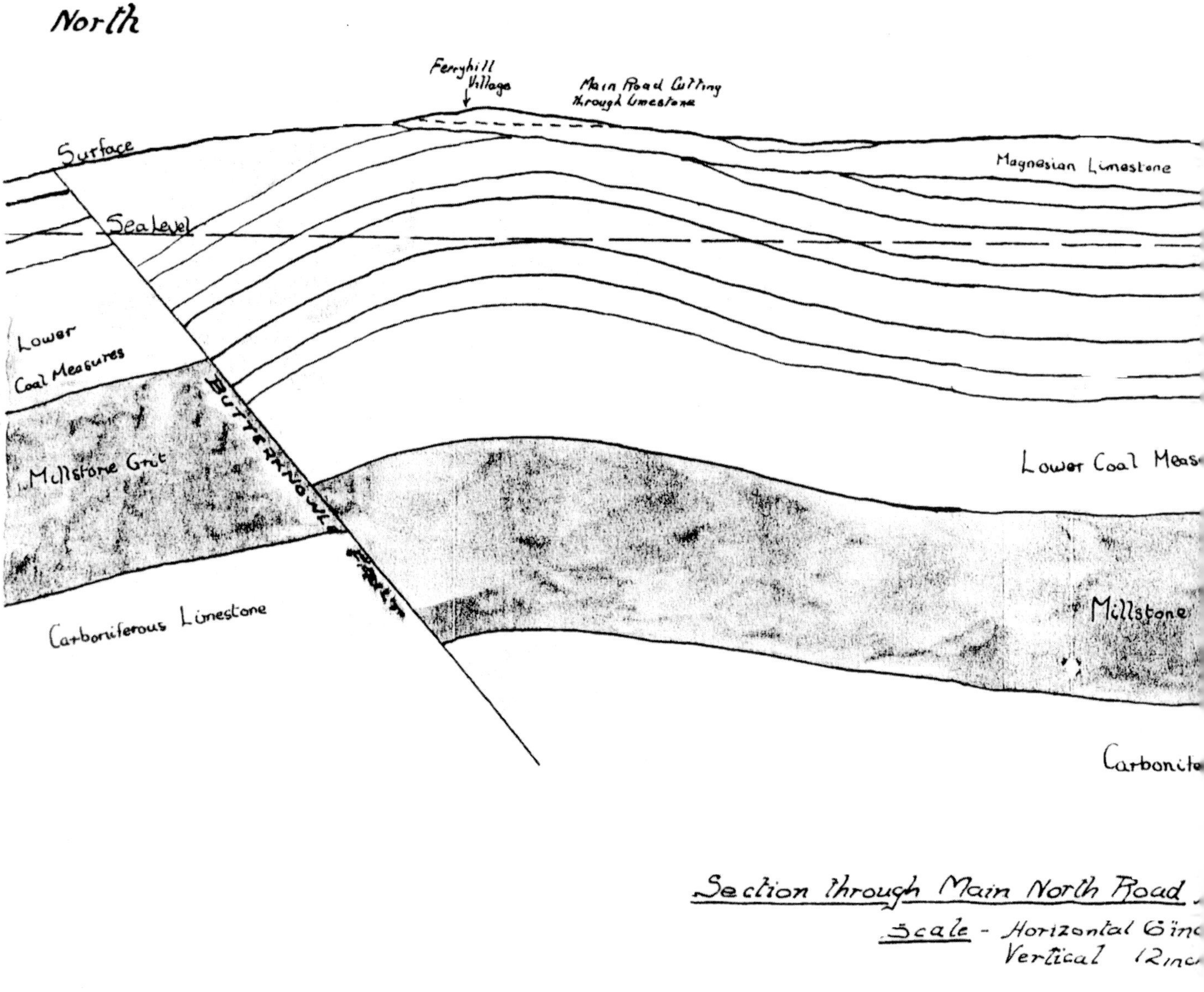

North

Ferryhill
Village

Main Road Cutting
through Limestone

Surface

Sea Level

Magnesian Limestone

Lower
Coal Measures

BUTTERKNOWLE FAULT

Millstone Grit

Lower Coal Meas

Carboniferous Limestone

Millstone

Carbonit

Section through Main North Road

Scale - Horizontal 6 inc
Vertical 12inc

30

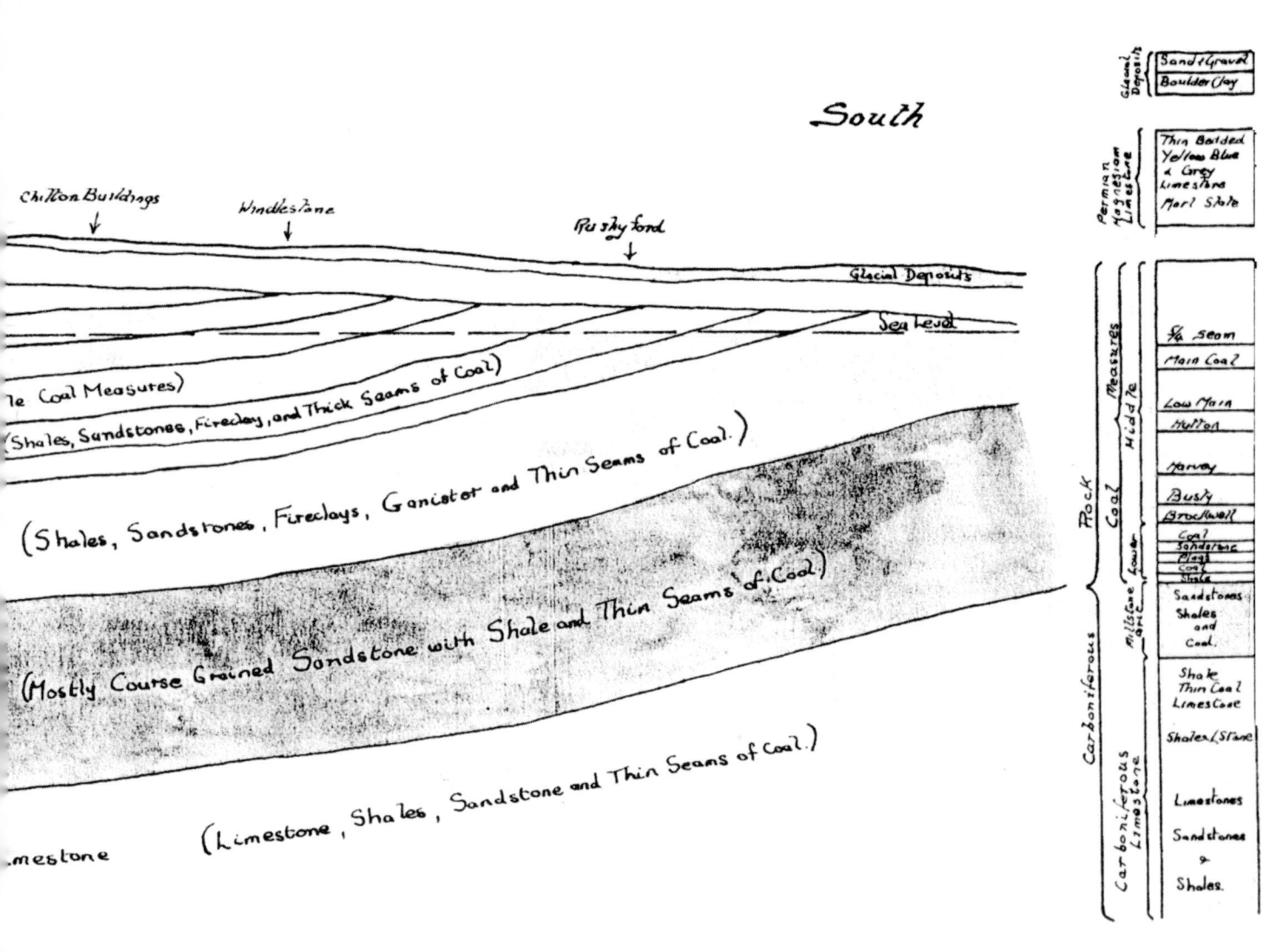

South

Chilton Buildings — Windlestone — Rushyford

Glacial Deposits
Sea Level

(The Coal Measures)
(Shales, Sandstones, Fireclay, and Thick Seams of Coal)

(Shales, Sandstones, Fireclays, Ganister and Thin Seams of Coal.)

(Mostly Course Grained Sandstone with Shale and Thin Seams of Coal.)

(Limestone, Shales, Sandstone and Thin Seams of Coal.)

...mestone

| Glacial Deposits | Sand & Gravel |
| | Boulder Clay |

| Permian Magnesian Limestone | Thin Bedded Yellow Blue & Grey Limestone Marl Shale |

Carboniferous — Rock

Coal Measures — Middle
- ¾ Seam
- Main Coal
- Low Main
- Hutton
- Harvey
- Busty
- Brockwell
- Coal Sandstone Plate Coal Shale

Millstone Grit — Lower
- Sandstones Shales and Coal.
- Shale Thin Coal Limestone
- Shales & Stone

Carboniferous Limestone
- Limestones
- Sandstones & Shales.

Rushyford to Ferryhill

1 Mile Approx
1 Mile Approx

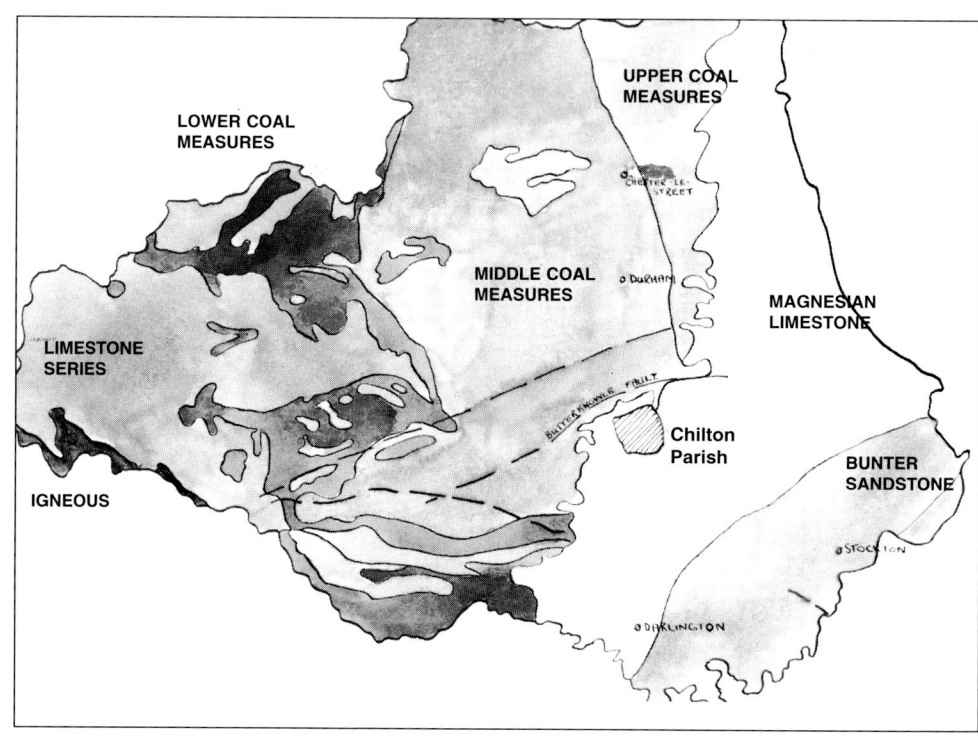

Durham County geology

Durham County geology (shown left) shows that the Coal Measures in the centre and east are overlaid with Magnesian Limestone. The Coal Measures stratum, dipping to the sea, is composed of more than twenty seams of coal, varying in thickness from ten inches (25cm) to over six feet (l85cm), with various layers of sandstone and shale separating them. The Permian deposits form the East Durham Plateau and consist of an upper bed of Magnesian Limestone, in some places up to 700 feet (215m) thick a middle bed of Yellow Sands, varying from 0 to 150 feet (46m) and a lower bed of impervious Marl Slate.

The Magnesian Limestone, which is almost concealed by drift deposits, outcrops (ceases to exist) to the north and west of the parish, and the same occurs to the north-east at Trimdon, leaving Chilton situated on the Magnesian Limestone.

The coal seams all climb to the south-east and come to an abrupt halt (the incrop) when they reach the Magnesian Limestone. The deepest workable seam, the Brockwell, incrops into the limestone south of Rushyford where the Durham Coalfield ceases to exist.

Therefore, Chilton and Windlestone were fortunate to have their industrial development. Had the coalfield finished two miles further north, a village totally different to the one we have today would have evolved, with a very different heritage.

Windlestone Colliery

Sinking the pit shafts 1873-77

Joseph Pease and Partners of Darlington secured a lease to work coal from Sir William Eden, Baronet, of Windlestone Hall. The approximate area to be leased (the royalty) began at Leasingthorne roundabout to the west and stretched to Kay's Hill Farm in the east, the northern boundary being a line drawn between these two points. To the south, the royalty followed a wandering line running to the south of Kay's Hill, Woodham Lodge, 250 metres south of Rushyford, then along to Rope Moor road ends, before heading north-west over to Windlestone Hall and Leasingthorne roundabout. This wandering line also represents, in geological terms, the "incrop" where the

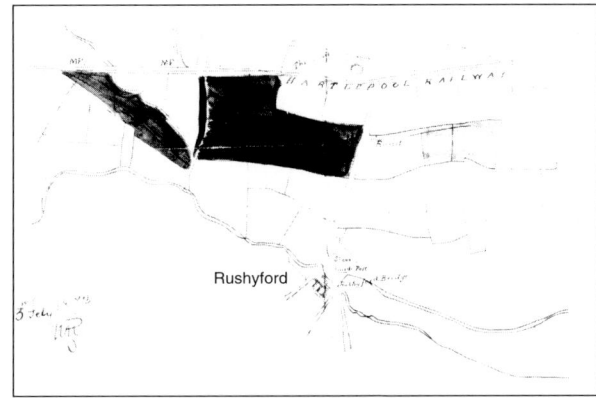

Plan 1 showing the first proposed siting of Windlestone Colliery dated 3rd February 1872 (enlarged for greater detail on page 43)

Brockwell seam ceases to exist, and which is, in fact, the southern edge of the Durham Coalfield.

The term of the lease was for 63 years, commencing July 15th 1871 and the area covered 1380 acres. Other minerals included in the lease were, fireclay, for brick making, and ironstone, used in the manufacture of iron.

At first, it was decided to sink the pit shafts some 200 metres to the rear of what is now Chilton and Windlestone Workingmen's Club, next to Mill Wood, commonly known as the Plantation (Plan 1). The railway sidings for this site were to go further over to join the

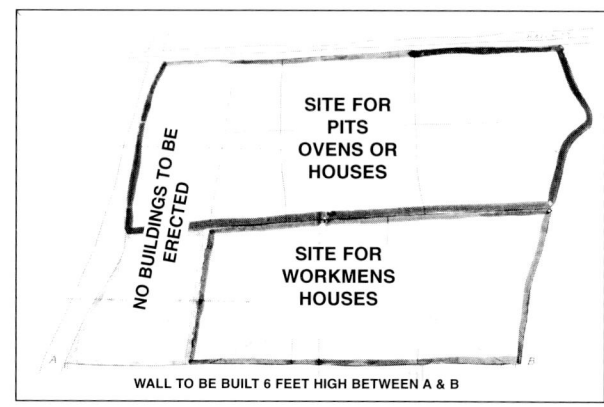

NO BUILDINGS TO BE ERECTED

SITE FOR PITS OVENS OR HOUSES

SITE FOR WORKMENS HOUSES

WALL TO BE BUILT 6 FEET HIGH BETWEEN A & B

Plan 2 - shows the location agreed upon, the appropriate areas are highlighted, as described in the Memorandum Alterations. (enlarged for greater detail on page 43)

West Hartlepool Railway, a total of 400 metres from the Great North Road. The railway had, by this time, changed its name. One can only assume it changed hands from the previous owners, Clarence Railway Company. The plan to sink pits at this location was scrapped. A Memorandum of Alterations to the original lease, dated 15th October 1872, moved this new venture (Plan 2) to the site where Chilton Junior School now stands.

For the first three years of the term, the rent was £3000 per annum, afterwards £4000 per annum, for the privilege of working an equivalent quantity of coal. The tonnage rent thereafter to be one shilling per ton of twenty hundredweights, on all coals drawn to bank. The fireclay and ironstone to be 6d per ton, each.

It may be of interest to cast an eye over the following memorandum alterations:

Memorandum of Alterations, which has been agreed by Sir William Eden, Baronet, and Joseph Pease and Partners, shall be made in the Memorandum of Terms for the Grant of the Windlestone Coal Lease, made between them and dated February 3rd 1872.

1. Paragraphs 9, 11, 12 and 13 in such Memorandum of Terms and the **Plan 1** attached thereto, are, and shall be wholly cancelled, and the following paragraphs shall be taken as duly inserted.

   Those numbers 9, 12 and 13 in place, and in lieu of those, the numbers of which correspond, on **Plan 1**

9. Lessees to have the power to sink pits, erect heapsteads and shops, make railways, build coke-ovens (which shall be flued) and fireclay works and otherwise to exercise all the usual and necessary powers over the surface within the limits coloured round with red on the annexed **Plan 2**, (the coke ovens to be placed as

near to the railway as practicable) except that no erection or building shall be placed to the west of the dotted line, running north to south on the said plan.

12. Lessees to have the power to build such houses as they may require on the land coloured round with blue on the annexed **Plan 2** and on such part of the land coloured round with pink on the said plan as lies to the east of the said dotted line and to have the land lying to the west of the dotted line contiguous to the last mentioned land and coloured round with yellow, as the garden ground, but no erection or building to be placed thereon.

13. The land held under paragraphs 9 and 12 to be at the rent of £3 per acre per annum, at the expiration or sooner determination of the lease, all houses to be built on any part of such land as shall have been used or occupied within five years, to be left for the lessor in fair tenantable repair.

   All other parts of the said land to be restored fit for agricultural purposes, or compensation paid, for injury done by such want of restorations.

13. Lessees to build and during the lease maintain in good and sufficient repair and leave at the expiration or sooner determination of the lease in the like repair, a wall six feet high from the surface of the land between the points A and B, shown on the annexed **Plan 2.**

14. Demise. And thereto and all the coal and Fireclay and Ironstone within and under these six fields or parts of fields, recently part of the Chilton Estate and abutting onto the Chilton Branch Railway which the said Sir William Eden has lately acquired from the Earl of Eldon.

15. And thereto and in addition, one hundred tons of best round coals at the option of the lessor for such use as aforesaid, and such coals shall also be free of rent.

For Self and Partners in the Firm of Joseph Pease and Partners

J. W. Pease.

15th October, 1872.

Taking a Chance

Sinking pits on the southern edge of the Durham Coalfield could be uncertain and speculative in nature, with Windlestone and Mainsforth Collieries coming into this category. The site of Mainsforth pit was on the east side of the east coast main railway line at Ferryhill Station, where some of the original surface buildings still stand, forming part of Mainsforth Industrial Estate.

The main reason for their problems was a bed of Magnesian Limestone about 200 feet (61.5m) thick and generally of a permeable nature. Where any considerable thickness of this type of limestone is sunk through, there is certain to be a great amount of water. In the sinking of Windlestone shaft, they met with water feeders at intervals down to 550 feet (169m); one such feeder, at 800 gallons per minute, burst in at 394 feet (121m).

Mainsforth Colliery, only three miles away, had Magnesian Limestone about the same thickness as Windlestone. I have no account of the water met with, it may well have been a much larger quantity than at Windlestone, as it ultimately led to the closure of the pit.

These two collieries were not alone. At most of the collieries in the Magnesian Limestone district, the water has been the major difficulty the shaft sinkers have had to contend with. It caused the greatest outlay of capital at Silksworth, Wearmouth, Whitburn, Ryhope and Seaham pits, some of these pits pumping up to 1000 gallons to the surface every minute.

At Windlestone, the first sod was cut to start sinking the shaft on 21st March 1873. The first six feet were achieved in twenty-four hours. It took another four years to reach the Brockwell seam. Shaft sinking continued through a number of thin coal seams. This group of seams below the Brockwell is commonly known as the "lower coal measures" and were generally regarded as not worth working in this area. Sinking stopped on 13th October 1877. A further 193 feet (59m) were bored from the shaft bottom, but no more coal was found.

A Costly Error

I have two copies of the strata sunk through at Windlestone, shown here in this diagram. The First Section is from Robert Calvert's "Geology and Natural History of County Durham".

The Second Section is one I came across among some old papers belonging to Tommy Buckle of Windlestone.

The First Section shows the results arrived at during the actual sinking of the shaft, the first named seam being the Main Coal at 313 feet (96.3m). As the sinking progressed, the sinkers met with a number of seams at intervals,

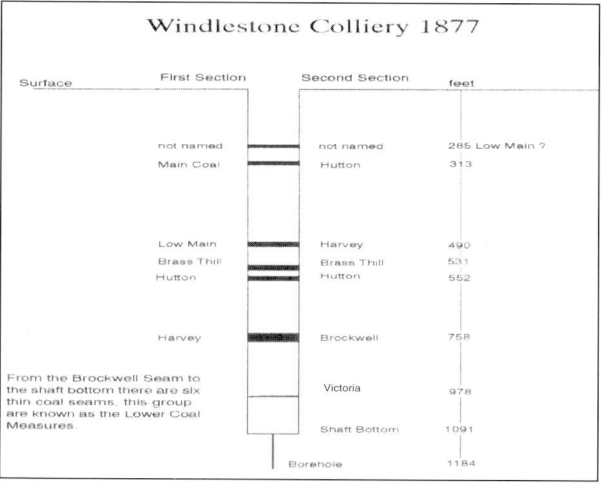

Windlestone Colliery 1877

Surface	First Section	Second Section	feet
	not named	not named	285 Low Main ?
	Main Coal	Hutton	313
	Low Main	Harvey	490
	Brass Thill	Brass Thill	531
	Hutton	Hutton	552
	Harvey	Brockwell	758
From the Brockwell Seam to the shaft bottom there are six thin coal seams, this group are known as the Lower Coal Measures.		Victoria	978
		Shaft Bottom	1091
		Borehole	1184

and eventually came to the Harvey Seam at 758 feet (233.2m).

With the Brockwell seam, six feet (1.85m) in thickness and apparently of good quality, below this point, sinking continued to 1091 feet (335.7m) with a further 193 feet bored.

The Second Section shows the first named seam to be the Hutton Seam at 313 feet (96.3m) and the Brockwell at 758 feet (233.2m).

The Brockwell was worked extensively at Windlestone for the whole period of the pit's life, at a depth of 758 feet. The Second Section looks to be correct; in so far as the Brockwell is concerned, it appears that the geologists at the time of sinking the pit were unsure and got it wrong in 1877, the extra sinking of the shaft below the Brockwell level and the further boring being unnecessary and costly.

The Colliery Village

There would be no time lost commencing coal production after the lengthy sinking operations. Miners working at this new pit needed somewhere to live, resulting in the building of Windlestone Row.

A separate community of three streets in line was built on the land now covered by trees and shrubs between the end of New South View and Prospect Terrace. Access to the Row would be an unmade road to the rear and, to the front, a footpath. The end houses of each street were larger than the rest to accommodate those responsible for the day-to-day running of the mine, the remainder were smaller houses for the miners and their families.

Windlestone Row was not very grand; however it was home, and houses were not easy to come by. They consisted of two ground-floor rooms, a kitchen/living room with a large cast iron combination range with a coal fire in the centre, an oven for cooking on one side and a cast iron pot (a side boiler) on the other. The second room, the parlour or front room as it was often referred to, was used only for visiting relatives or special occasions.

Upstairs were two bedrooms: the main room to the front had a dormer-type window and the room to the rear had a severe "T" fall roof, the wall only three feet high from floor to ceiling, with a small window built in, giving very little light.

Water initially came from a series of wells put down to the rear of the houses. It was many years later that mains water was installed, just a single tap through the wall at bucket height.

Without mains water there were no flush toilets, only an earth or ash closet, across the back yard, a small building adjoining the coalhouse. A strong disinfectant, Thymo Cresol, was distributed free, to kill any bacteria. The closets were cleaned out once a week by raising a sliding plate to the rear, in the back street. Council men using shovels loaded the contents into a cart or wagon with covers or doors on the top and closed them immediately the work was complete. Food and other provisions, as well as household coal, were all delivered by way of the back street. One or two of the houses doubled up as a shop, selling groceries and hardware - John Brown worked at the pit, his wife ran the shop at No.74.

Windlestone Row, later to become South View, about 1880s. The big house, No.1, would be the Colliery Manager's house.

The Depression

The Coal Depression, responsible for the closure of Windlestone, affected Chilton Pit, with its closure in the mid-1880s. Mainsforth Colliery was sunk to the Harvey Seam at a depth of 857feet (261.3m); by 1877, it closed without any coal being worked. Water, the amount of capital outlay and the depression were the main reasons for abandoning the project.

Little Chilton Colliery closed about 1890 in this case, the coal reserves were exhausted.

Going back a few years, the West Hartlepool Harbour and Railway Company owned a number of pits, one of them being the Bull Crag Colliery, situated midway between Great Chilton and Little Chilton farms, on the right side of what is now a public footpath. This pit closed about 1870.

By the 1890s Chilton Buildings was almost deserted, the early years of coal mining not amounting to very much. What had appeared to be a promising start had become a bitter disappointment, with the community dying on its feet.

An indication of how little was going on is borne out by the parish records at Ferryhill. From 1890 to l900, Chilton Buildings was only mentioned twice.

The first time was in the form of a letter, drawing the council's attention to:
"the insufficient supply of water at the cottages of Chilton Buildings, owing to the pumping machine being out of order".

The second being:

"A settlement of 3/- (shillings) per week, to be paid to the Chilton Buildings' lamplighter".

Finally, in this same period, there was no mention of Chilton Buildings in the Parish Register (Ferryhill parish) and it was only mentioned once in 1900.

Many of the miners and their families had moved on to other pits which were working and, if they were lucky, a house with the job. Travelling, for the miner, meant walking to work and there was a limit as to how far a man could walk everyday with no other form of transport available. He needed to live as near as possible to the pit where he was employed.

It was a poor start for Chilton and Windlestone, which consisted of little more than two rows of colliery houses, Dene Bridge Row and Windlestone Row; the Chilton Buildings Board School, built in 1878, and the houses which made up Chilton Buildings; and a number of houses named "The Square", to the rear of the Wheatsheaf.

Times could hardly be worse. Those who remained had few or no prospects and unfortunately it remained that way for many years until the turn of the century.

Windlestone Colliery about 1908 taken from a position near the entrance to Chilton Junior School

Windlestone - the Good Years

The pit stood idle for 22 years before it was given a second chance, opening in the early part of 1906. Pease and Partners, who owned Windlestone, also had Eldon Colliery, to the rear of Close House, at Gurney Valley.

This second chance brought about a major expansion in house building, with New South View completed by 1907.

New South View with South View (formerly Windlestone Row) further on, Shelley Terrace opposite, one of the first built by the Council.

These houses were of a similar design to those houses at the bottom of Eldon Bank, which Pease seemed to favour. They were for the officials of both collieries who were in charge of the day-to-day running of the pits. The detached house in New South View, now the vicarage, was the colliery manager's residence the next house, No.2, belonged to the undermanager; and so on along the street, with overmen, deputies, surveyors and engineers occupying the remainder. The Colliery Institute, with its pebbledashed walls, bears the same Pease's trademark and is mentioned later on.

The spate of house building continued, extending to Prospect Terrace, Arthur and Albert Streets and Windlestone Colliery Institute by 1916. The second half of Albert Street, the last to be built during the First World War, became home to a number of refugee families from Belgium, fleeing the German advances across their country. The street got the nickname "Belgian Street", with the head of the house, and any person old enough, working at the pit.

This expansion coincided with a similar one to the north of the railway line, at Chilton Buildings.

Eldon had been working the Brockwell Seam for many years in an easterly direction towards Windlestone, and finding it more costly and difficult the further their workings progressed from their own shaft bottom, to say nothing of increasing problems with their ventilation.

With a pit shaft sunk down to the Brockwell and the seam virtually unworked, Pease saw the viability in reopening Windlestone and, in the greater scheme of things, could foresee a a time when Eldon would be coupled to Windlestone underground.

1906 to 1924 saw a steady rise in coal production and, without doubt, the best years for the mine, working the 6 feet thick Brockwell and, from 1922, the Harvey seam. More miners were taken on, the good times were back and, whilst it was hard work, they would all be saying "thank the Lord".

A new coal-screening plant, together with extra railway sidings to accommodate more trucks, gave a picture of prosperity the like of which the residents of South View thought would never be possible. With more than 300 colliery houses occupied, there were probably more than 400 men and boys working at Windlestone by 1918.

The mine worked to the west and a little to the south in the general direction of Windlestone Hall, keeping well clear of the area known as the Incrop, where the seam, climbing at an inclination of 1 in 5, met the water-bearing limestone.

OS Map: Pre-1930 The Brockwell Seam
(Shown in greater detail on Page 42)

Underground at Windlestone

It may seem, at times, that there is a lot to understand when looking at mining information. Description and explanation are kept as simple as possible and minor details left out. The pits play a major role in our story: this being so, it is important that the reader has the information at hand, to make of it what he or she will.

A plan of the Brockwell Seam at Windlestone (shown on page 42) illustrates the extent to which the workings have gone. If one looks closely, the mine workings are overprinted onto a plan of the surface area.

l. Leasingthorne workings are to the top left behind the thick, shaded line (the barrier). Chilton,Windlestone and Eldon to the west worked the remainder. **The heavy black lines denote the main roadways underground.** eg. Look at the circle with a cross inside it, next to the "W" of Windlestone Colliery. This is a pit shaft. From the shaft, a heavy black line runs west and a little to the south. This is a main roadway, 233 metres below the surface.

2. The black lines, forming squares, are also roadways.

3. The white squares formed by these black lines are solid coal and known as pillars, left in to support the roof stone above the coal seam.

4. The dotted line, at approximately 45 degrees at the bottom right of the plan, is the "Incrop".

At this point the Brockwell seam ceases to exist and the Durham Coalfield ends.

The Brockwell Seam as
explained on Page 41

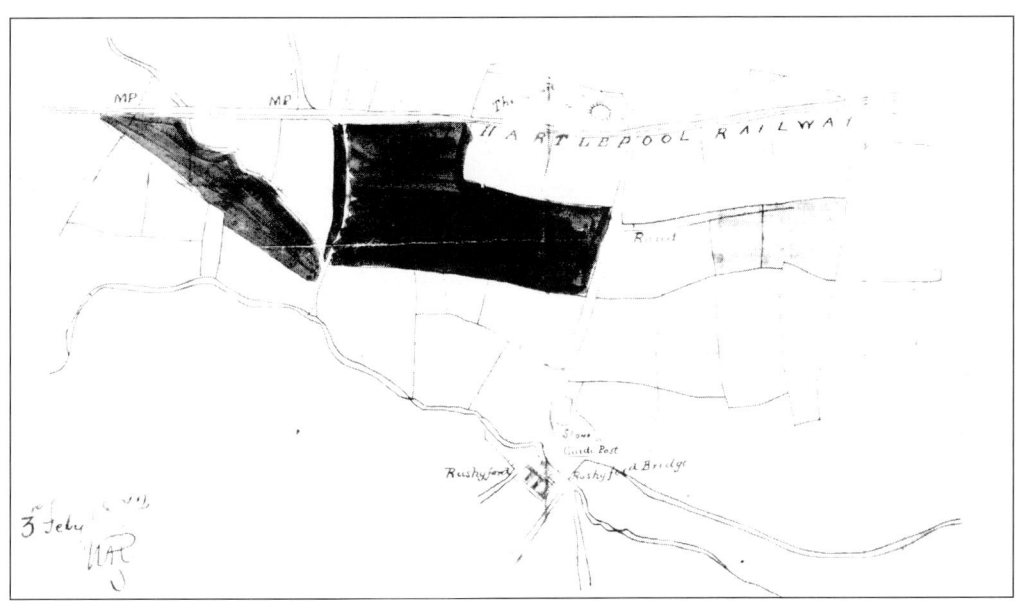

Plan 1 - (as described on Page 33)

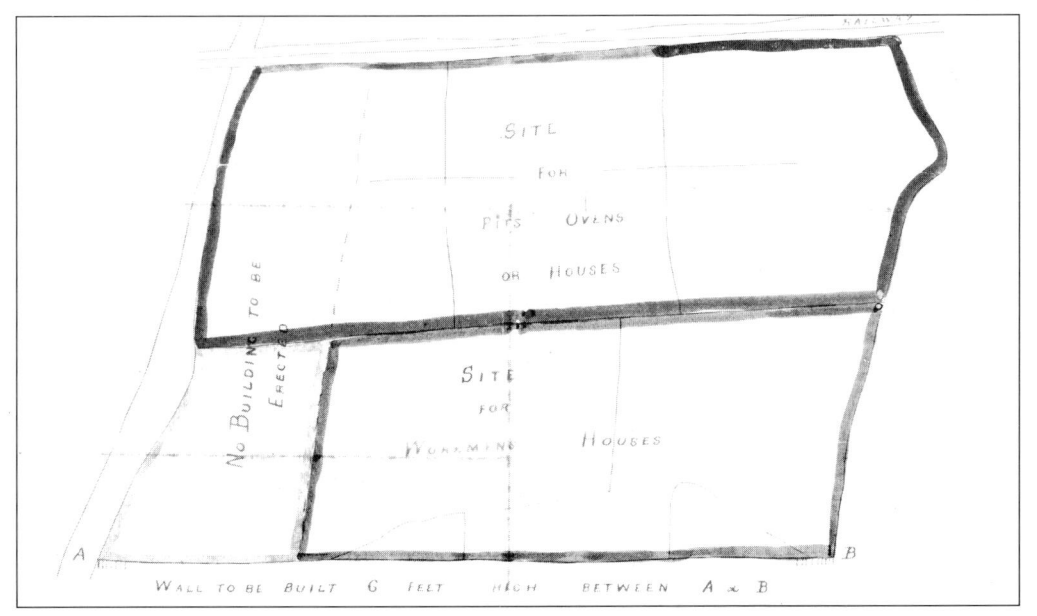

Plan 2 - (as described on Page 34)

Coal Hewers

The coal hewer

One group of men who contributed to the companies' profits were the coal hewers. Mining companies knew the importance of good, skilled coal hewers. The man himself had to be fit and resilient; he was the man with the handpick who used to hew the coal. His other tools consisted of a big hammer, the head weighing as much as 12 pounds, used to knock up wooden props under planks, as tight as was possible, to keep the roof up and make his place safe to work in. A large, round-shaped hand shovel (pan shovel) had evolved, making forward penetration under the coal he had hewed much easier when filling into a tub. Our hewer of 1900 is seen working in poor light with a soft hat and no protection for his knees. It appears to be quite warm, hence the shorts.

In this thin seam of coal, the hewer is laid on his side with a gruelling task to perform. If water were to seep from the roof or floor, it would make no difference, he would carry on. At the back of his mind he would be thinking of the air coming into his place, was there enough to breathe and was there enough to keep away the miner's invisible enemy, GAS. Firedamp (methane) could explode, it only took a spark, or it might be blackdamp (carbon dioxide) with no oxygen it would not support life. All these things gave the hewer plenty to think about, there was no time for daydreaming.

A more recent photo only goes to highlight the fact that little had changed in 80 years. The coal is higher and this coal hewer is wearing a helmet, kneepads and an electric cap lamp, enabling him to see wherever he looks. Even so, it was still hard work.

The average working hours in 1906 were high. A report sent from Chilton Colliery to the Durham Coal Owners' Association revealed that miners worked eight-to-twelve hour shifts. Most worked over 50 hours per week with only Sunday off. In 1909, the average became 55 hours. Some trades worked longer, especially those not regulated by the Factory Acts. There was a privileged exception, consisting of the Deputies who ran the mine underground, coal hewers and those with exacting tasks to perform such as shaft maintenance personnel. Their average hours were less.

The hand putter

Hand Putting

The criteria for a hand putter were in many ways the same as for the hewer. He had to be fit, strong and not without a fair amount of skill, when he had tubs full of coal to push around all of his shift.

Putting tubs where they were needed is a good job description. The putter is working by candlelight in roadways not much higher than the tub. For the duration of his shift of eight hours or more it would be doubtful if he got to stand up straight at any time. Putters had a sixth sense when it came to pushing tubs around in the semi-darkness. As the tub wheels passed over the joints in the rails, he knew each one. Some of them were out of alignment due to rotten sleepers caused by water running and an uneven bottom. He would twist and turn the tub, left or right, to keep it on the track. If the tub was derailed when it was full and quite often weighing more than half a ton, he had to lift it back on to the track on his own, and backbreaking work it could be.

Compressed Air Picks

This pick, used by the coal hewer, with its continuous "bat-bat" action could loosen the coal much quicker and easier than the hand pick. It was in common use at many of the mines

during the 1900s. With the CA pick available to the hewer, he had to produce more coal for his pay. The "windy pick" was its local name, they were used extensively at Chilton and Windlestone and are still used to this day in other mines. The number in use has fallen dramatically with the decline of the coal industry but there will always be a place for this tool so long as mining goes on, especially in the small drift mines still dotted about the UK.

Chilton banner

The Durham Miners' Association, the union representing the miners at collieries large and small throughout the Durham Coalfield, now had branch officials selected by the men to look after their interests. The branch was more commonly referred to as the Lodge. Chilton and Windlestone lodges were on hand to hear of any complaints or grievances, of which there were many in those days against what can only be described as tyrannical and ruthless coal owners of the 1800s and 1900s.

Banners, Bands, Pits and People

Lodge banners were eyecatching, full of colour and would often depict champions of their cause with most of them carrying a few well-chosen words to convey solidarity, such as "Unity is Strength". The banner was a symbol, something physical to relate to and rally round. It was a boost to their confidence, something they needed plenty of in those days. They were immensely proud of their Association. The women and children were instinctively affected by the men's struggle and their support was automatic.

The brass bands of Chilton and Windlestone were catalysts in bringing the whole community together. Their music could be light and cheerful, heartwarming and inspiring, even religious, and was many things to many people. The band was capable of catching the mood and able to reach the souls of all who listened, whether it be a sad or happy occasion.

Windlestone Colliery Band about 1914-18. **back row 2nd left:** *Tot Dixon (flugal horn) picked out by son Bob of Jade Walk* **middle row far rt:** *Tommy Welburn (tenor horn) was a pensioner of The Grove in 1942* **front row:** *Bill Campbell (big drum),* **to his left:** *Mr.Longstaff (euphonium)* **far rt:** *Jimmy Banks (trombone) who lived in South View*

Windlestone Band held their practice sessions in Jack Hunter's hut, on his allotment at the bottom of Prospect Terrace. Chilton Colliery Band used the Union Room (now demolished) for their rehearsals; this building was adjacent to the Wheatsheaf pub. As with many bands of this era, they were, for the most part, made up of miners working at that pit, and were always in demand, playing at fund-raising events and football matches, and giving concerts in the Institute and the Club.

Brass band competitions kept them busy. Not unlike football, there was friendly rivalry, whoever progressed the furthest bringing the comment, "Hey lad, our band's better than yours ever was!" Of course, the highlight of the year had to be playing the banner into Durham City on Gala Day.

One may wonder where the names come from to fit some of the faces on the old photographs. This was made possible with the help of Sam Keenan and others, some of them former miners, who congregate in a small lounge bar in Chilton Club nicknamed "the Vatican", on a Friday evening. Sam, a former miner who spent many years at Chilton Pit as a pieceworker and union official, lives in Windlestone.

Collectors for the National Relief Fund September 1914

The small gentleman wearing the straw boater (hat) to the left of the pit pony is Jimmy Rochester, undermanager at Windlestone Pit. He lived in No. 2 New South View, the official house for his position at the mine. In his retirement, Rochester became caretaker of the Social Centre, a building of wooden construction at the rear of 10/11 New South View. It was used, as the name suggests, for all manner of meetings and social functions and, in later years, was known as the Labour Hut. He was one of my boyhood memories, a little old man who always smoked his cigarettes in a holder. In his prime he would be the hirer and firer at Windlestone Pit, a person to fear and respect.

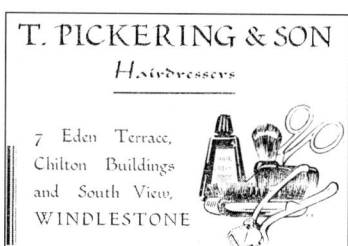

Separate Identities

The residents of Windlestone were those living on the south side of the old railway on land mostly owned by the Edens and were known locally as "Windlestoners". To the north of the railway they were Chiltoners, with that area belonging to Lord Eldon. Each community was proud of its own roots, as it should be.

The name of Windlestone seemed to decline with the pit closure and the demise of the Edens and, for a while, it was missing from the postal address, although it seems to be making a comeback in recent times. Windlestone, rich in history. Not only for being the seat of the famous Eden family, but also for all those who live there, we should ensure the name is not lost as so many things can be, in the name of progress.

Brought about by the expansion of two mining communities, the residents of Chilton should always be aware of those who may want to forget the name of Windlestone, one of the cornerstones of our heritage.

Progress 1910-20

The growth of the two villages, now rapidly becoming one due to continued expansion, were no longer dependent on the land for a living. But, surprisingly, Sir William Eden still remained powerful and dominated the area as much as ever. By the end of 1910, the miners were beginning to take an interest in their power as a community. Although as yet they were not organised, they were learning about their rights.

It was obvious to many that a clash between Sir William Eden and the miners was inevitable as the miners became more politically aware. On December 6th 1911, Chilton Parish Council applied for an additional district councillor for Chilton Buildings ward.

The population was now 4000 with a rateable value of £20,000 and they were not fully represented. Chilton Buildings was a young and undeveloped village in 1911, with a background of relative calm at the mine. The following years saw an enlarging of its social and commercial activities.

It also continued to expand throughout this period, but at a much slower rate.

The school attendances give an accurate guide to this, since it only increased by ninety children in nine years and even showed a decrease from 1913 to 1919.

School attendance: 1910 pupils - 730, 1911/12 - 753, 1913/14 - 824, 1918/19 - 819.

Windlestone's Gala Day

The biggest occasion of the year for any colliery band is the Durham Miners' Gala in July. Up at the crack of dawn would be the band and the branch officials of the union, accompanied by a number of men and women only too keen to help. Two of the men had their names drawn out of a hat to carry the poles of the lodge banner. For these men it was a great honour. The band, its musical skills honed to perfection from weeks of practice in Jack Hunter's hut, were ready for the big day.

Windlestone Colliery Band with miners and some of the ladies, with their banner, at The Big Meeting 1920/22

The miners, some accompanied by their wives and families, along with many others all dressed in their Sunday-best clothes, would be ready and waiting for a well-earned day out. A happy family day out, where few would deny anyone a drink of beer, a walk around the stalls and a sit on the grass for a picnic on the old racecourse down by the river at Durham. There were the platform speakers, some of these eminent politicians of the early 1920s, such as Ernest Bevin, who became Foreign Secretary in 1949, and J. Ramsey MacDonald MP. These and many others who championed the cause for better conditions for the miners would be listened to and given standing ovations after their speeches.

Above, a cross-section of Windlestone folks are seen with the colliery band and the lodge banner. A special photo for one to keep in those days, with the local MP alongside union and colliery officials, all present for the big day.

"Gala Day" the ultimate occasion for the miner and his family.

A group of very proud, hardworking men and women, here to enjoy a day out. More names to fit the faces are as follows:

Bowler hat, in front of the banner: *John Herriotts, who became Member of Parliament for Sedgefield in 1922* **right of Herriotts:** *Joby Reed* **3rd from Joby:** *Bill Joyce of Prospect Terrace* **4th from the right** *"Luggy" Etherington (trombone) with only one ear* **2nd from the right: (sitting)** *Jimmy Banks (trombone)* **right of the drum:** *Tommy Meek (cornet)* **left of drum:** *Jack Hirst* **the lady, 2nd left: (sitting)** *is Tommy's mother, Mrs. Meek.*

*Windlestone Colliery Institute built in 1908,
now the Catholic Church opened in 1947*

The colourful atmosphere in Durham City on Gala Day is unique. In the 1920s, with so many pits working, the streets were packed from side to side from the New Inn and the Market Square to the Racecourse. Banners were paraded and bands played all manner of different tunes, with young people dancing a jig as they moved along. It was still like that when I attended my first Gala in 1949 at the age of 15.

The miners had come a long, hard road and the price had been high. In the 1920s, there was still a long way to go. As history shows, they did eventually achieve the conditions of work and decent pay they had always fought for.

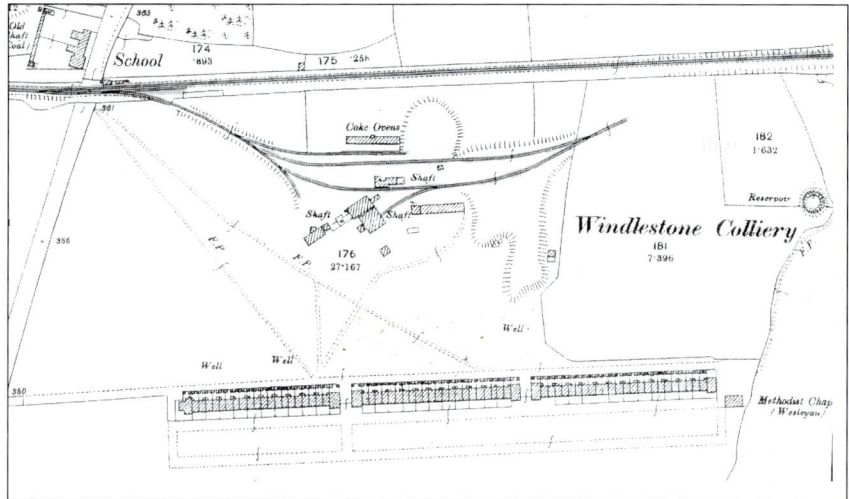

Windlestone 1906 shortly after the mine was reopened and before any expansion took place

The Colliery Institute

The Institute, attractive in design even to this day, was built in 1908. One can imagine the many hours of enjoyment it gave to the men, women and children of the village.

At a time when most people were hardworking, with not too many creature comforts to brag about, the Institute was a boon and an ideal place for the community's leisure activities. Concerts, dancing, wedding receptions and meetings were held in the main hall. A reading room with daily papers and a library were there for the use of the members, as well as a sports room. It was a much-needed asset. Even though Pease and Partners exacted their pound of flesh from the miners, they were quite proud of their new amenity.

In 1924, John Brown of 74 South View, was the secretary of the Institute. In their spare time, he and his wife ran a grocer's shop in part of their house. John was short and stocky, with a walrus moustache and a pull-down trilby hat. He was often seen wearing leather leggings from the top of his boots to his knees, as worn by many, such as farmers, butchers and milkmen in those days. He always appeared grumpy with a scowl on his face, but then, he probably had good reason if any of us kids were knocking about too near his ponies, tethered out the back of his house on the field next to the pit where he worked. The slag heap was not much further away, not that it bothered anyone, they were used to it.

The rules of the Institute were quite simple and straightforward. They were as follows:

1. All persons using the Institute must pay 2d (old money) per week. Boys under 16 years ld per week. The money will be collected when the union money or unemployment money is paid.

2. Each member must show his card whenever asked by the Caretaker, Committee or Secretary.

3. No person will be allowed to sign on, or draw unemployment money or union money in the Institute, except fully paid-up members of the Institute.

Bob Jordan, a resident of Mill Cottages, situated half a mile from the Eden Arms on the Bishop Auckland road, was quite a character. In his eighties, he used to cycle from Mill Cottages to Chilton Club most weekday lunchtimes and sometimes the odd evening. He was a slightly built man with a rather big mouth, made bigger with no teeth in it. Wearing two or three days stubble on his face and a flat cap, he was a rare sight in his long raincoat. He liked a pint of beer and used to sing in the bar with a few of the old retired pitmen.

Bob liked a bit of fun and was never one for trouble. He kindly gave me a Windlestone Colliery Institute subscription card for 1924/25, from which the previously written rules were copied.

The Durham Miners' Association (DMA)

The Early Days

Mining, never the easiest job, was, from its starting point, hundreds of years ago, up to the 1900s, slave labour for almost everyone.

The coal owners operated a harsh set of rules to ensure maximum profits. There was little sympathy for anyone stepping outside the guidelines. For instance, evictions were the order of the day for miners causing unrest amongst their workmates.

In this kind of environment, with the majority of miners subservient and without direction, there came together small groups of dedicated and courageous men. They were determined, at whatever cost to themselves, to better the lot of the miner.

These men, usually miners, with support from others closely allied to the mining industry, were well aware of the task they had embarked upon. The struggle for recognition is well documented by Alderman John Wilson JP in his "History of the Durham Miners' Association 1870 to 1904".

Windlestone Colliery Institute Subscription Card for 1924/25, John Brown, Secretary

The first Miners Deputation 1872

back row l - r: *N. Wilkinson (Treasurer), W. H. Patterson (Vice President), M. Thompson, T. Ramsey, G. Jackson, J. Forman*

front row l - r: *W. Askew, W. Crawford (President and Secretary), J. Handy, T. Mitcheson*

In the early days, these brave men held meetings, often in secret, for fear of reprisal against those who helped them. These pioneers, who were no strangers to being knocked about themselves, doggedly pursued their goal and, with time and patience, brought about the birth of a creditable force which the miners desperately needed to represent them, namely the Durham Miners' Association. The first deputation from the Durham Miners' Association to the Coal Trade Office in Newcastle-upon-Tyne, was held on February 17th 1872.

The Coal Trade Office was formed from a previous body known as the Durham Coal Owners' Association, and this was also their first meeting. Their Chairmen were, respectively, Hugh Taylor and William Stobart. There were twenty representatives for the employers and ten delegates from the DMA, representing 20,000 workmen.

The miners' leaders at this time were: W. Crawford-President and Secretary, W. H. Patterson-Vice President, N. Wilkinson-Treasurer. The remainder of the delegation were:

M. Thompson, G. Ramsey, G. Jackson, J. Forman, W. Askew, J. Handy and T. Mitcheson. There have been many since that time who have carried on the fight for better conditions for the miner; the list is a long one. Some of those who come to mind easily are those depicted on the union banners, which we can still see paraded at Durham on the Miners' Gala Day. Kier Hardie, Peter Lee and A. J. Cook are some, closer to home, John Herriotts of Chilton championed the union's cause and, as a local Labour politician, was elected Member of Parliament for Sedgefield.

The First Gala Day

The first in a long series of meetings took place in Wharton's Park, Durham, on Saturday 12th August 1871. For sometime prior, district meetings had been held in different parts of the county and great efforts were made to secure a good gathering on this their first Gala Day.

In addition, a sum amounting to twenty pounds was offered, in three prizes, for a band contest, and liberal money prizes for various athletic sports. There was a charge for admission, and it was estimated that between 4,000 and 5,000 paid to be admitted. The speakers outside the Association were A. MacDonald, W. Brown (Staffordshire) and John Normansell (Yorkshire). The local speakers were Mr. W. H. Patterson, Mr. Hendry (Addison Colliery) and Mr. Ferguson (Edmondsley). The platform was decorated with the Thornley banner, and in the arena was a banner bearing the inscription, "A fair day's wage for a fair day's work".

The Chairman was Mr. W. Crawford and his first words were:

"This is the first great Gala Day of the Durham Miners' Mutual Confident Association, and I only pray it will not be the last."

He reminded them that he and his colleagues had only been trying to organise the county. They had met with great difficulties but they were still alive, and more likely to continue alive than ever. *"I can assure you," he said," that on this, the 12th day of August 1871, the Durham Miners' Association was never in a more healthy position, never more healthy, with its regard to its feelings and determination to carry on its great work of organising the county.*

Never more healthy with respect to its funds and never more healthy in reference to the general progressive tendency of its operations, since the first day the Association had been established." The speakers were men who did great work in the Trades Union Movement in the period ,with which we are dealing. One notable speaker from outside the county, William Brown from Staffordshire, had peculiar methods, partaking more of a religious revivalist. He often opened meetings at home with a prayer and had a small collection of songs entitled "Melodies and Poems" from which he would sing before he commenced speaking. At this first gala, Brown sang two of these songs and recited the following poem:

Working Men.

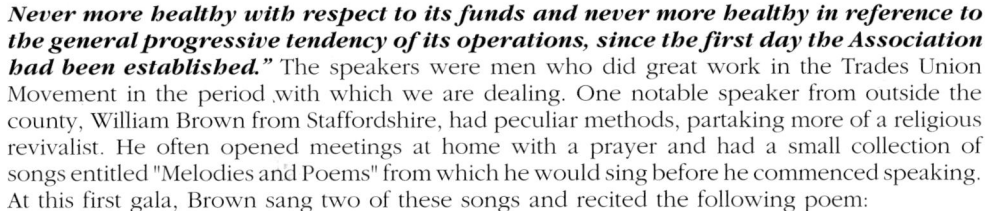

Think what power lies within you,

for what triumphs you are formed;

Think but not alone of living,

like the horse from day to day;

Think, but not alone of giving,

health for self, and soul for pay;

Think, oh! be machines no longer,

engines made of flesh and blood;

Thought will make you fresher, stronger,

link you to the great and good;

Thought is a wand of power,

power to make oppression shrink;

Grasp ye then the precious dower,

Poise it, wield it, work and think.

These men, heroes of the highest order, who inaugurated one of the finest series of labour meetings ever held in this or any other county, who saw the possibilities which lay within us, and who spoke such words of hope, have all passed to their reward. A reward, which awaits the good and true, who battle for the right, in whatever clime or sphere of life.

Their spirits still live and move and have being in many today, bearing testimony that "The good men do lives after them".

Mrs. Mary Robinson, a Miner's Daughter

William Thompson (Slaughter, wearing his Sunday best in 1934

I called on Mrs. Robinson, who was living in 20 The Poplars, Chilton, while her son, Bob, an old friend of mine from my school days, was here from New Zealand, where he lives. I had enquired of Bob, who was visiting for a few weeks, if I might ask his mam about the old days in Windlestone. Mrs.Robinson readily agreed, once asked, and the following is her story.

"I was born in 1909 and we lived at Cleatlam, near Staindrop, and I went to school in Staindrop for a while. My father, William Thompson (Slaughter), worked at Winston Pit. The two rows of houses where we lived belonged to the pit. Our family moved to Windlestone when father was recommended for a job by Mr. Rochester, the undermanager at Windlestone Pit, in 1915. We moved into 41 Albert Street. The first six houses had been given to the Belgian evacuees, it being during the war, 1914-19, and only half of the street was built.

At this time, the German Zeppelins (air ships), were looking to bomb Hartlepool and we were put in the cupboard under the stairs for safety. Father worked as a *stoneman at Windlestone Pit and he had the reputation of being a good worker. He was a hard man with no patience, a bad temper on occasion and liked his pint of beer. I asked my mother, "how do you put up with him?" She replied, "better the devil you know," and added, "where else could I go?" "How did he come by his nickname, Slaughter, "I enquired. "He always kept a shotgun," she replied. "He had a reputation for shooting vermin, rats, foxes, anything that the local farmer or smallholder wanted rid of. They would call on him if they were overrun. Father had two allotments at the bottom of Prospect Terrace. The vegetables, eggs and the odd chicken helped to keep the home going, especially through the pit strikes.

There was a "knocker up" who came round round the streets to knock people up for work. The time to get up was chalked on the wall, next to the front door.

When I was just a girl I went to the pit for father's pay note every Friday.

Eddie Loftus lived in 39 Albert Street. He was a *driver at the pit. He had an accident at Windlestone Pit, underground. He was only 15 years old and was killed.

With little money about, mother used to go to Ferryhill Market late on a Friday afternoon to buy fruit when it was being sold off cheap.

I was given ld a week pocket money on a Saturday so that we could go to the picture hall. The "Star" picture hall was in Durham Road, next to Richardson's chemist shop (now Roots). Mrs. Scrafton, also of Durham Road, used to play the piano accompaniment during the showing of the films,which were silent in those days.

My sister and I used to go to chapel three times on a Sunday. One Sunday, the Salvation Army Band was playing through the streets of Chilton. We followed them into their hut (now the St. John's Ambulance) and watched the service. When we got home, we got a good hiding for going in.

Taking stone from above or below the coal seam to increase the height of a roadway.

During the 1926 Pit Strike, the children at the Big School next to the church were given a banana each and soup was dished out from buckets by the miners who were on strike."

Mary Robinson's mention of soup being dished (served) from buckets is shown to good effect

Taken in Chilton Council School yard next to St. Aidan's Church. Most of the people here are miners on strike from Chilton and Windlestone pits in 1926. The pick and shovel have been swapped for buckets, wooden spoons and ladles to serve hot soup to the school children. Proud and obviously willing to do his bit is Twi Mason, wearing a pinafore.

Standing left to right: *Mr. Stewart, Andrew Kennedy* **5th left:** *Bill Pearson, then George Swinbank, Michael Wright (Councillor), John Herriotts* **3rd rt:** *Twi Mason* **far rt:** *Ric.Pearson* **Sitting, in the centre:** *Mr. Raynor (Headmaster)* **far rt:** *Fred Allison (Codger)*

*The Driver worked underground, usually along the main roadways, which were the furthest away from the shaft bottom and referred to as "right inbye". From the inbye landing, where the roadway had been made wide enough to accommodate upto 40 empty tubs on one track and 40 full tubs, on a similar track alongside, the driver, using a pony, would take as many empty tubs as the pony could manage, taking them further inbye to the putters. He would then bring their full tubs back to the landing to be coupled together.

CHAPTER FOUR

Chilton Buildings

Chilton Buildings

The hamlet of Chilton Buildings, in the early 1800s, consisted of a small group of houses and a public house named the Duke of Cleveland, and was situated on the "Great North Road", less than a mile north of the crossroads at Rushyford, eight miles south of Durham City and ten miles north of Darlington.

To the east, within two miles, are Chilton Hall, Great Chilton Farm (once the home farm of this estate) and Great Chilton Cottages. From here, along Gypsy Lonnen, is Kay's Hill Farm; a little to the south and a mile or so to the east, Chilton Grange. The road leading from Chilton Buildings, in their direction is known as Chilton Lane. Finally, one mile to the north of Great Chilton Farm is Little Chilton.

The history of the Chilton area is no less interesting than Windlestone. There is much to say and many pages could be written, enough to fill a book on its own. In dealing with the last 175 years, I find it necessary to delve a little. In doing so the first people involved in our industrial heritage appear, Christopher Mason and Lord Eldon.

It appears that Bishop Hatfield granted free warren (access) to Great Chilton and area, including the isle of Bradbury, to William de la Pole. In 1388, this area was part of the forfeiture of Michael de la Pole, when the King, to pacify Bishop Skirlaw for his having seized the forfeited lands, granted him the custody thereof. It does not appear that the de la Poles held the manor.

Alicia Heron and husband, John, succeeded to the manor from the Earl and Countess of Lincoln, who died without issue. Alicia also had possession of Little Chilton. From then, the area was successively the property of the Bowes of Dalden, the Blakistons and the Halls of

Chilton Hall, home to many of the previous landowners of the Great Chilton Estate. After Christopher Mason, William Bacon, part-owner of Little Chilton Colly. occupied the Hall for some years.

Great Chilton Farm House. The style of the chimney stacks and the general design may well date the house at more than 250 years old. Bill Shields worked this farm in the 1940s-70's.

Newsham. A moiety (half) of the manor was conveyed by the Halls to John Jeffrayson and John Morland, who immediately conveyed it to John, Lord Bishop of Durham. This part of the estate eventually passed to the Greenwells and Duns.

The other half of the estate passed from the Blakestons, through the Wildes and Millbankes, to Christopher Mason and the Reverend Robert Waugh, in 1798. Mason lived in the mansion house, Great Chilton Hall. He increased his holdings by paying £3,400 to Mary Betcherly and Ann Wetherall for land close to his own.

Reverend Robert Waugh sold his part to Sir Vane Tempest, Bart. It then became the property of John D. Lambton and, subsequently of Lord Eldon.

Christopher Mason

Mason was a long-time breeder of stock, with a good eye for business and the right beast. In 1810, he obtained a pure breed of improved Durham shorthorns. The prices offered and refused for some of his breed were enormous. For one cow, MARCIA, Mason, in 1807, refused 800 guineas. CHARLES, a bull of the same breed, was let for the highest sum ever obtained in England, £450 for two seasons.

Great Chilton Cottages, situated between the hall and the farm, built to house employees of the Estate or the Farm.

Lord Eldon

It was just before the death of the first Earl of Eldon in 1838 that the modern exploitation of his Eldon and Chilton estates' coal reserves began, which bordered Eden's estate on three sides: to the west, Eldon; on the north side, through the middle of Chilton Buildings; and on to Nunstainton in the east.

He had been born John Scott in 1751, was knighted in 1788, created Lord Eldon in 1799 and Earl of Eldon and Viscount Encombe in 1821 (Encombe being a former name of the Wheatsheaf public house). The reason for this sudden rise in the social world of a Newcastle hostman's son, was being his extremely successful practise of the law which led, among a number of other factors, to his appointment as Lord High Chancellor of England and his holding that office during periods 1801-06 and 1807-27.

With part of the fortune he acquired, Sir John Scott (as he was known then) bought the manor of Eldon and 1300 acres for £22,000. By the time he had purchased Nunstainton prior to 1873, the then Earl of Eldon owned 11,841 acres in County Durham.

The Eldons and the Edens effectively owned all of the land on which Chilton and Windlestone are built. There being coal underneath, it would make the coal owners wealthy and the landowners even more so, without lifting a finger.

In the 1820s Mason was involved in the prospecting for coal on Lord Eldon's estate at Dene Bridge. Coal had been mined in the south-west of Durham for centuries, production being restricted due to a limited knowledge of ventilating the workings, and to the absence of engineering skills to get the coal out to the surface. Transport in those early days was ancient, by horse and cart, or wagon, and roads were little more than rutted tracks.

In the late 1820s there was a distinct possibility that the Government would authorise the construction of branch lines into the Chilton and Ferryhill districts. With this major development about to take place, the exploitation of coal reserves in the Chilton area took on a new meaning. Collieries with big tonnages were envisaged if the railways were built, giving easy access to the port at Teesside where coal could be shipped relatively cheaply to the markets of London and the South.

So it was no surprise to see Mason having a borehole put down at Dene Bridge to ascertain the coal seams which lay beneath the surface. Dene Bridge became the site of the first Chilton Colliery and Mason the first owner, the pits name, Great Chilton Colliery.

A pit shaft, bearing Mason's name is to be found on Ordnance Survey plans of Chilton. It is sited 70 metres to the rear of the old Chilton Board School, last used by Sedgefield Borough Council as a training centre. One record shows that he worked a seam of coal a little over one metre thick at a depth of 86 metres from the surface. Although Mason would not be aware, there being little in the way of geological information to go on at that time, his venture, to say the least, carried a fair amount of risk.

The modern-day mine plans show that this shaft was sunk almost on the edge of the Durham Coalfield where a number of coal seams cease to exist. This could well have accounted for the poor quality of the coal met with, as well as faults which can displace the coal seam, upwards or downwards, causing it to disappear. Finally, water seeping into the workings was not uncommon to the district. The pit closed in 1835, all the colliery plant and equipment being sold in October of that year.

Great Chilton Colliery at Dene Bridge also failed, the year 1835 being a personal disaster for Mason. He died shortly afterwards.

It appears to have been a bad time for all concerned, and a poor beginning for any expansion at Chilton Buildings.

Kay's Hill Farm House during the 1970s

Kay's Hill Farm House 1999 extensively altered, both inside and out, by the present owner Ed Murray over the last 20 years. Originally two houses, dating from the 1700s.

Clarence Railway Company

In 1833, the Clarence Railway Company obtained the authorisation needed to construct branch lines and commenced work on its Chilton Branch. This was completed to Great Chilton Colliery in 1835, by laying a three-quarters-of-a-mile section to reach the Dene Bridge site, from its main branch. This main branch extended west to Leasingthorne Colliery, Coundon and the Westerton area. Here, pits such as Westerton and Byers Green had opened some years earlier. This branch was completed to its terminus, at New Coundon, in 1836.

It must have been a great blow to Clarence Railways when Great Chilton closed, with the pit largely unproductive for the few years it existed. The track to Dene Bridge was taken up.

At Little Chilton, Mr. Thomas Arrowsmith obtained a lease to work coal, from the Bishop of Durham. They were working a seam of coal named the Five Quarter, its thickness approximately 1.5 metres, at a depth of 76 metres from the surface. Little Chilton village being a mining community in its own right, situated close to Ferryhill Station, boasted its own Colliery Mechanics' Institute established, in 1850 with up to 70 members. There were from 700 to 800 well-assorted volumes in the library, costing upwards of £100. Here, lectures were given from time to time.

Clarence Railways constructed a branch line from Ferryhill Station to Arrowsmith's Colliery in 1834. By 1850 the line had changed hands, the West Hartlepool Harbour and Railway Company being the new owners. They were hauling Little Chilton's coal to the West Hartlepool Docks for shipment to the South of England. In 1872, this branch was extended west by way of a tunnel under the Great North Road, in the dip north of the West Close, then on to Chilton Colliery at Dene Bridge.

High Hopes

In 1872, some thirty-seven years later, trial borings of the Five Quarter seam indicated once again, that there was a possibility of working Lord Eldon's coal at Chilton economically.

A lease was proposed or granted to a group of businessmen consisting of John Straker, John C. Straker and Jos. H. Straker (who were probably related),and John Henderson, the term of the lease being 56 years from November 1871 at a minimum rent of £4000 from the fourth year. The leased area at this time was for 1200 acres, with tonnage rents at 10d for the Harvey and Brockwell seams, 8d for the other seams of coal and 6d for any fireclay, immediately above or below the seam, used in the manufacture of house bricks. A *barrier of solid coal was to be left in, next ti the adoinng Royalties.

John Henderson MP lived in Durham City and John Straker at Tynemouth. These two gentlemen, along with others, were also partners in Eldon colliery, situated on the hillside, north of the present brickworks at Eldon. Henderson was also a partner in a large pit in Yorkshire, named Sharlston, while the Strakers had interests in Brancepeth Colliery.

These were powerful men, with the finances to take out a lease and develop pits, knowing

Barrier Coal: The width of solid coal (60m approx) left in to separate one royalty/ lease from the other.

that mining was not a certainty, but willing to take a chance, for what could be a bonanza return on their investment.

Shaft repairs at No. 2 Pit began in in 1872 at Dene Bridge, the site of the previously failed venture of the 1830s, with the royalty now covering 2000 acres. A new Shaft No.1 Pit being sunk 15 feet in diameter (4.6m) to the Main Coal and continued at 10 feet diameter as a ventilating shaft to the Brockwell seam. The No.2 Pit, sunk at 15 feet diameter right down to the Brockwell, this seam lying at a depth of 1200 feet (369m). Coal production began in 1875 and the first miners' houses, Dene Bridge Row, were built about this time. There had been a boom in the coal trade, but a depression was not far away and, although the pit opened with an increase in the population of the village, the depression continued, the effects of which were felt very deeply. In 1883, notice was given to terminate the lease, and the pit was shut down in 1884. A sale of the plant was held, but none was sold and there were no takers for the lease. Lord Eldon, the landlord, was responsible for the maintainance and repairs at the closed mine. To keep it in a condition so as to lease it again should times improve he spent £42,000 mainly on shaft repairs. The major difficulty was the circular shaft wall, which was constantly on the move and giving way. Installing *tubbing (explained on page 64) into these sections was done with great difficulty as other walled sections were in a poor state and likely to collapse, making the work doubly hazardous.

Chilton Colliery remained closed until 1900. All the surface plant was sold off eventually, with the exception of the vertical steam winding engine, with twin 36-inch diameter pistons, and a Cornish pumping engine.

By that time the houses at Dene Bridge had become completely dilapidated. Dene Bridge Row are the oldest miners' houses in the village, built in 1873 for Straker and Henderson who took up the lease

Dene Bridge Row

to sink Chilton Colliery in 1871. The mine was sited 250 metres to the rear. With the exception of the pitmen who lived in Dene Bridge Row, the remainder walked or cycled down the backstreet and round the bottom corner before fanning out to all parts of the village. Well over a 1,000 men, six days a week and black as the ace of spades. A very common sight, over 50 years ago.

*Tubbing

Heavy cast iron segments 18 inches (.46 m) to 36 inches (.92 m) deep, there being eight to twelve segments in a complete circle. The first ring of tubbing is the "foundation ring". It sits, located, on another tightly wedged ring, a "wedging curb". This wedging curb protrudes into the circular pit shaft, forming a smaller diameter, allowing the foundation ring to sit on it.

Rings of tubbing are then built up from this point, until it has risen beyond the deteriorated area of shaft sides causing the problems.

Chilton Colliery 1884-1900

This plan from 1897 shows the mine buildings with no railway access, only the road travelled by the pitmen on their way to work. This road is still in evidence to the rear of 22 Dene Bridge Row. The dotted lines stretching away from the buildings to top right indicate where the railway sidings used to be, from 1872 until 1884. The Engine House housed the haulage engine used for pulling trucks up the gradient from Little Chilton to Chilton Pit through a tunnel under the Great North Road, in the dip north of West Close.

A Time of Change

The South Durham Coal Company of Wallsend-on-Tyne, were working Eldon Colliery prior to 1900. They also had Chilton, but made no attempt to open it up. Chilton had been closed since 1884. There were a number of serious enquiries about the mine, including one from Bell Brothers the Iron, Coal and Lime Masters

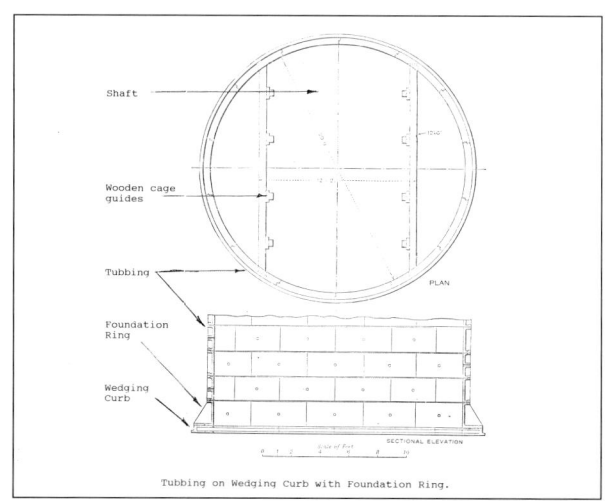

Tubbing on Wedging Curb with Foundation Ring.

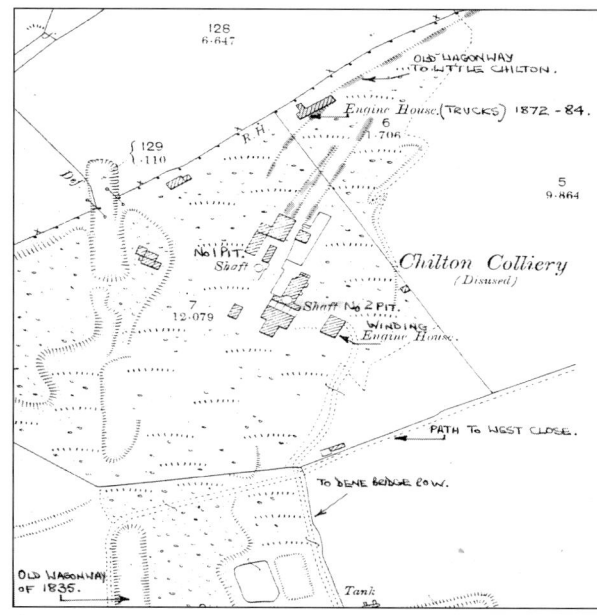

of Middlesbrough, who commissioned a report in 1897 into the viability of the Chilton royalty, with the outcome being far from favourable.

It was reported that Chilton, and also Mainsforth for that matter, which adjoined, lay on the extreme south of the Durham Coalfield and had already had some £500,000 spent on them. Both collieries were sunk in the worst possible place for winning coal underground; in short, there were quite a number of good reasons against the speculation of more money on either of these pits. Bells were unable to decide on this new development, and they were not the only ones to be hesitant, which was understandable in view of the report.

The year 1900, however, was to be a significant year of change, brought about by a mining company who could foresee possibilities at the closed Chilton Mine.

Mr. Stobart, representing Henry Stobart and Co Ltd, whose head offices were at Etherley across the road from the Dog and Gun public house, enquired if Chilton Pit might be to let. He eventually secured a lease for 42 years, at a rent of £500 for the first year, then up to £1500 in the third and following years. Stobart had decided to take a chance, and he was not to be disappointed. Chilton Buildings and Windlestone were to become major beneficiaries.

Eldon Colliery appears to have filtered into our tale. It was sunk in the early 1800s to the Brockwell seam at a depth of 967 feet. Water migrated from the outcrops and the surface rivers in the west of the county, flooding the workings of closed pits and eventually finding its way to Eldon shaft bottom. This involved the need to pump an ever-increasing volume of water to the surface to keep the pit open. Although this pit is not central to our story, nevertheless it was to leave a legacy in future years which both Chilton and Windlestone pits could well have done without.

Lord Eldon's agents and Stobart had to resolve a major problem before contracts could be completed on Chilton - the dereliction of the colliery houses. They included Dene Bridge Row (74 houses) and 9 at Chilton Buildings. This was not all; there were more houses at Chilton Lane, comprising Chapel Row, West Row, Cross Rows, Railway Row and Upper Railway Row. Most of these had been unoccupied for a long time. Some of the houses at Chilton Lane had been built too close together and, to satisfy new sanitary regulations, some were knocked down. Most of the houses mentioned here, needed roof and floor repairs. One can imagine the run-down state of these two communities and the living conditions that those families had to endure.

It is unlikely that the houses at Chilton Lane were involved in the terms of the contract for the reopening of Chilton. Their position lay between, and nearer to, the now closed Little Chilton and/or Broom Collieries and the abandoned mine of Mainsforth. These houses were probably built at one time or another for these three pits, bearing in mind that houses would be needed at Mainsforth during sinking operations and the emerging possibility of coal production from 1875 to 1877.

Incidentally, in 1900 it was mooted that Mainsforth was to be reopened with coal production commencing by 1905. As a consequence, the houses in Chilton Lane would most probably be repaired for Mainsforth pitmen.

As it was, Lord Eldon laid out £10,000 for roof and floor repairs, presumably at Dene Bridge and Chilton Buildings, while Stobart had the job of making the houses habitable, as well as paying £4 per year rent for each one.

It was a big step in the right direction, a shot in the arm, as they say. It would give a lot of people new hope.

SEAM	CONSISTING OF
Five Quarter	100 acres in pillars remaining to get
Main Coal	540 acres whole (solid) coal
	The above for household use
Harvey	40 acres only, had been worked
Busty	un touched
Brockwell	un touched
	The above are coking coals

The reserves of coal remaining in 1900

Henry Stobart and Company Ltd.

William Stobart and Co Ltd was probably the former name of this company, who were mine owners in the early part of the 19th century. A great number of their pits, from about 1850 to 1935, being in an area that Stobarts generally referred to as "Etherley and West Tees", covering an area from Evenwood to Bishop Auckland and to the north-west by Toft Hill and Etherley. The names of some of these pits are as follows:

Etherley "Jane and George" pits, situated close to the present-day Weardale Railway not far from Escomb; West Tees and Raily Fell at Ramshaw near Evenwood; Newton Cap near Toronto at Bishop Auckland, adjacent to the brickworks, still occupying the same site.

In addition, there were a number of smaller collieries also worked in the Etherley and West Tees area. Henry Stobart, who now had Chilton, would, in future years, add Fishburn and Thrislington collieries to his expanding company.

The above photo was taken after March 1902. Coal winding had commenced up No. 2 pit shaft, its headgear seen to the right of the chimney. Work was underway repairing and widening No. 1 shaft using the small wooden headgear, partially hidden by a cloud of steam, and at a time when the Staple Shaft was in use.

The Rebirth of Chilton Colliery 1900

The shaft walls of No. l and No. 2 pit had been deteriating for sixteen years, since 1884. Lord Eldon's efforts to keep them in reasonable condition, limited by the water level which, over the years, was slowly rising. On this basis, it is fair to assume that the collapsing shaft sides would accumulate as a pile of debris at the bottom of the shafts and nothing could be done about that.

The water level was well up the shafts by the time Stobart got involved. With repair work at No. 1 pit requiring a number of years to make it serviceable for ventilation and coal winding, Stobart decided to sink another shaft, mainly for ventilation purposes, from the Main Coal level down to the Brockwell level. This shaft was eight feet in diameter and known as a staple shaft. Fresh air is drawn into No. 2 pit. On reaching the furthest point of the workings, the air then returns to the surface, using the newly-sunk staple shaft, made possible by the large exhausting fan at the top of No. 1 pit. Pumping operations took priority, with the water up as far as the Five Quarter seam, 384 feet from the surface. As the water level lowered, it was then possible to commence the sinking of the staple shaft.

In 1902 the staple shaft was down to the Harvey seam with the water level just below it. Fresh air could now flow around these workings, allowing coal production to begin. In March of that year, the daily output was 250 tons per day. The condition of No. 1 pit shaft, above the Five Quarter level, was probably made serviceable in a short time, considering that some remedial work had been undertaken as and when necessary during the years of closure, it being above the water level.

Coal production commenced in the Brockwell Seam when the staple shaft reached that depth and fresh air could circulate around the new workings. Finally, the air flow made its way up the staple shaft to the Main Coal level and on along a connecting roadway to No. 1 shaft, the air, now foul (used), completed its circuit of the mine by being sucked up No. 1 shaft by the large ventilating fan and pushed out into the atmosphere.

The relation of the three shafts, one to the other, shown in the diagram, should help the reader understand how it was at that time. One thing is certain: a lot of arduous and dangerous work requiring great skill and care was done successfully to complete the rebirth of Chilton in those first few years with no one having an easy ride.

The Five Quarter and Main Coal seams had been worked prior to 1884. A confirmation of the Main Coal being worked at that time can be seen from this cutting.

A cutting from the time

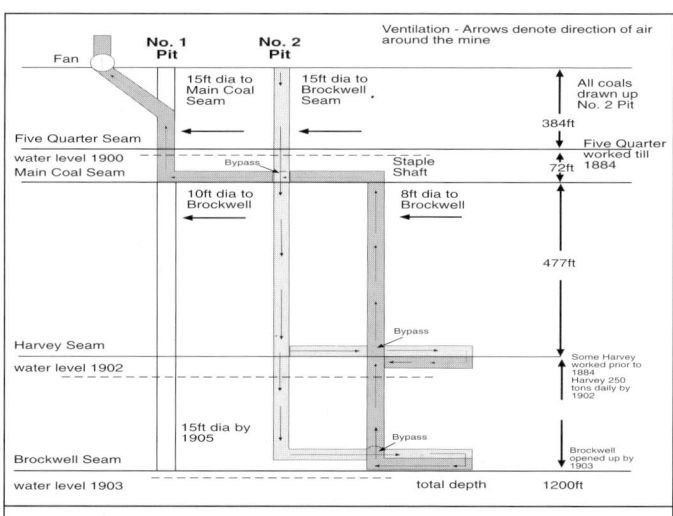

The Staple Shaft

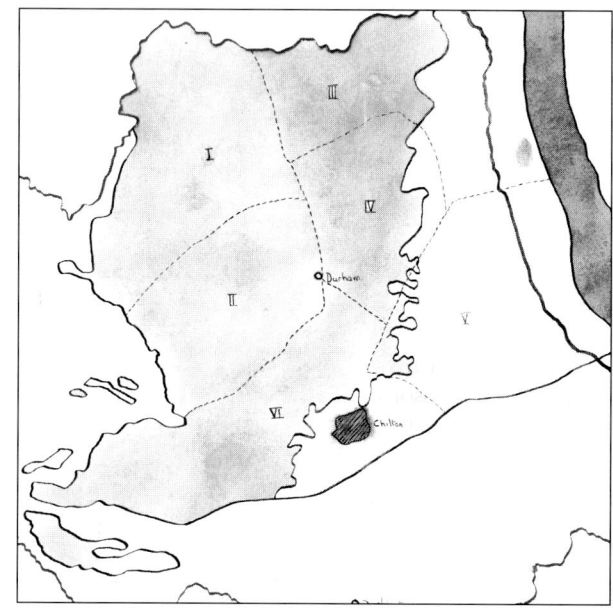

The final chapter of Chilton's rebirth, was the completion of the widening of No.1 Pit shaft by 1905. No time was lost in the erection of a new steel pit headgear to replace the old wooden one.

For the next twenty years or so, the Harvey and Brockwell seams were developed, with a ready market for coking coal and the by-products which were extracted from it.

When coal is subjected to the influence of a high temperature, a red or white heat, it is resolved into a series of volatile matters, described as gas, tar and water. A solid residue remains, containing carbon and other mineral matter. Its name is COKE. See this diagram for the general use of coal.

From 1900 to the 1921 strike was a relatively trouble free time. Local disputes apart, this was a fairly sustained period of good production, the reserves in the two seams mentioned being reduced apace, in line with demand.

The new latticed steel pit headgear (shown here) astride of No. 1 pit, nearing completion. Built in 1905 for Henry Stobart & Co. giving greater flexibility in the winding of coal, men and materials from the Harvey and Brockwell seams.

Top: Quality of Coal in the Durham Coalfields

I) Upper Seams - Gas & Steam
    Lower Seams - Good Coking

II) Upper Seams - Gas & Steam
    Lower Seams - Good Coking

III) Gas and Bunker

IV) Mainly Gas & Steam

V) Mainly Gas & Steam
    Remainder Coking for Blast Furnace

VI) Mainly Coking for Blast Furnace Use - some Gas & Steam

Bottom: The new latticed steel pit headgear of No. 1 pit

A constant demand for coking coal led to Stobart installing coke ovens at Chilton in 1907. A battery of fifty ovens were built by Fabry-Linard and designed to use 1600 tons of dry coal per week.

This coking plant required a chimney to be built, taller than the one presently in use for the boiler plant where large amounts of coal were also used to fire the boilers producing steam for the winding engines, compressors and various other steam-operated equipment.

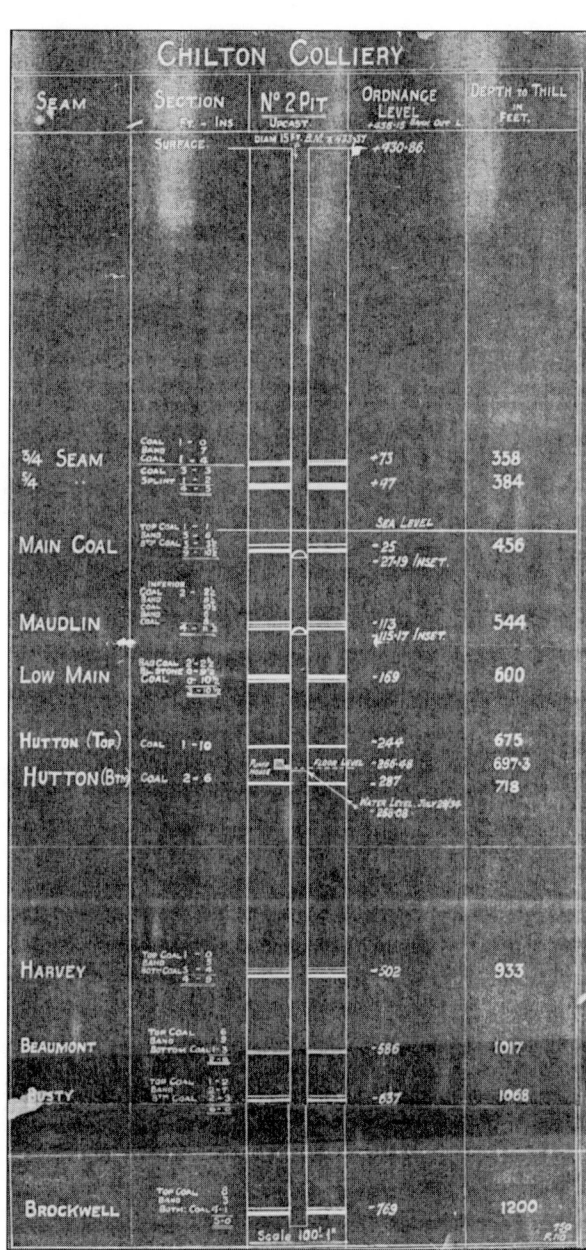

No. 2 pit showing the coal seams
and the depth from the surface

The new chimney of Chilton Colliery 1906/7

The new chimney can be seen here, partially built, located to the right of the No. 1 Pit headgear and a little above the eaves of the disused winding engine house.

Population Graph - Chilton Parish 1801-1991 as described on page 72

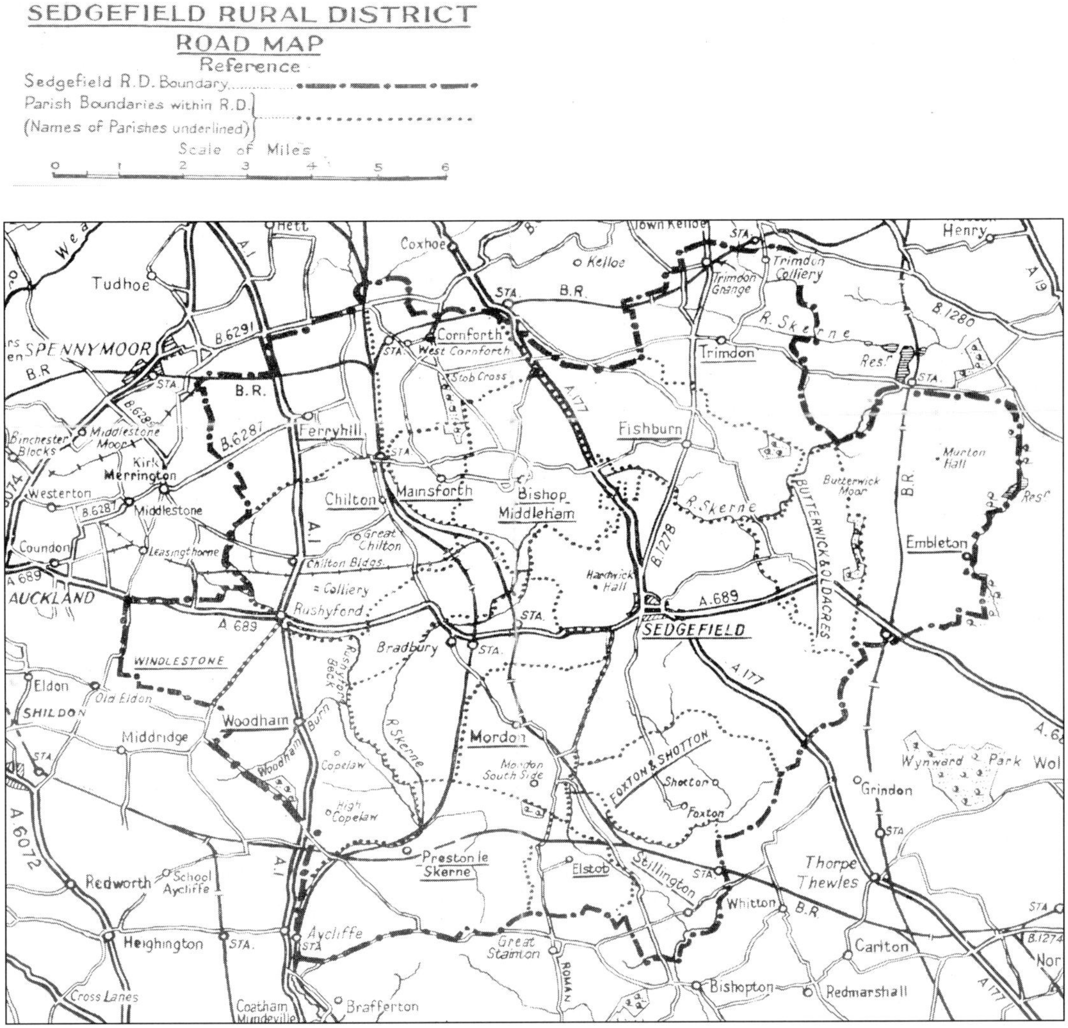

SEDGEFIELD RURAL DISTRICT
ROAD MAP
Reference

Sedgefield R.D. Boundary................
Parish Boundaries within R.D. ¦
(Names of Parishes underlined) ¦

Scale of Miles
0 1 2 3 4 5 6

Sedgefield Rural
District Road Map

Chilton Civil Parish

The Parish covered an area of 2422 acres, taking in Dene Bridge, Chilton Buildings, Windlestone Row and Chilton Lane. When referring to the population chart on page 70, in 1801 the figure was around 220. With the advent of mining in the 1830s, the population was up and down, following a trend closely allied to the success or failure of coal mining in the community. In 1871, the number was 643, mainly agricultural. By 1881 the figure was 2693, an increase of over 300%, the result of Chilton (1872) and Windlestone (1877) collieries being opened. Closure of both pits in the mid-1880s sent the population down to 1411. The Chilton Board School was built to take 200 pupils; the average attendance in 1890 was only 85.

Very little had happened to Chilton Buildings materially, since the 1820s, apart from the two rows of colliery houses at Dene Bridge and Windlestone and, of course, the school.

The "Stobart Era" would be the next to bring employment. Miners would say "thank you", but this work was at a price. For the miner worked long, arduous hours, and so did the young boys, for low wages. Not a lot to be thankful for, in other words, it was almost slave labour. There was one ray of hope for the future: the Durham Miners' Association, a union formed to improve the miners' pay and conditions of work - but even they found it to be a hard, uphill fight.

Chilton Buildings Board School (The Little School) built in 1878 serving the village for 92 years, the last infants moving to the school next to St. Aidan's (The Big School) in 1970.

A New Century, a New Beginning

With Chilton Pit reopened and once more producing coal by 1902, the expansion in the two communities of Chilton and Windlestone was to become meteoric, in the space of only ten years. The population was to rise from 1411 to 6070; this is supported by the baptismal and marriage records of the decade.

The increase in the populace had a knock-on effect on the school's attendances. From 1902/03, there were 121 pupils; by 1909/10 the figure was 648. It necessitated an extension to the Chilton Board School in 1908. This proved inadequate and a new school was built next to St. Aidan's Church in 1909.

Chilton Council School built 1909, the first headmaster being Sam Raynor

One of the elderly residents, Ernie Hope,who was 83 years old in 1979, wrote the following:
"In 1905, the Wesleyan Methodist Chapel was situated at the far end of South View near to Prospect Terrace, made of corrugated sheets. Durham Education had the use of it, for boys aged five to seven years, until the new school was built, next to the church in 1909.
I was one of the last boys to leave school at the Chilton Board School in 1909, after which it became the Infant School." *E. Hope 9/11/1979.*

With the prospect of a job and a house, the influx of miners and their families came from far and wide. Some of these were relatively local, moving from the west of the county where a number of the older collieries had closed due to the reserves of coal being exhausted.
There were others, such as labourers from the depressed areas of Wales, East Anglia, Scotland and Ireland, as well as the Cornish mining settlements. As the mine developed, the amount of coal raised at Chilton increased. In 1903, coal production was 66,634 tons; it then went up sharply to 173,000 tons by 1905. Five years later the figure was 277,000 tons annually.

W. SHAW
Beef, Mutton and Pork Butcher
SAUSAGES and PORK PIES
Fresh Daily
Horses and Cattle Bought and
Sold on Commission

CHILTON   FERRYHILL

Nathan Parkin

Durham Road

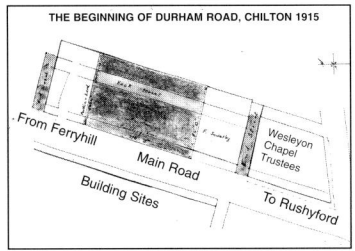

Beginning of Durham Road

What effect on Chilton and Windlestone?

In 1903, the place was completely unchanged from 1879. In 1904, the Parish Council records showed that an effort was being made to combine Dene Bridge Row, Chilton Buildings and Windlestone Row, by taking levels to ascertain the best way to deal with sewage problems, in the light of what was to come, a major increase in housing. In 1905, there was a constant mention of housing development, with building plans being submitted by the mine owners H. Stobart & Co.

The first street to be built was West Chilton Terrace, stretching from the main A167, along the road in the direction of Dene Bridge and the mine.

In the next three years, other streets were built, bridging the gap between Dene Bridge and Chilton Buildings, forming one larger unit. This was combined with a tremendous development of road works and road widening.

With the growth of the village, there was a corresponding growth of facilities. Private building of houses and shops took place and, as mentioned earlier, a new school was built, along with the Primitive Methodist Chapel in 1906. A. Jaques had his butcher's shop at 2 Eden Terrace, from around 1916. He purchased West Chilton Farm in 1929. W. Shaw's butcher's shop was next to the Board School. Both shops had their own slaughter houses to the rear where carcasses hung up on large hooks, a common enough sight then. By 1910, Chilton had grown to almost twenty streets, thirteen shops of various types, and one doctor. Thus, by 1909, Chilton was beginning to exert an influence upon its district in many ways.

Parkin and Lord

Nathan Parkin, stonemason and builder, lived at Copley near Butterknowle. A good craftsman, Parkin was responsible for building some of the attractive stone houses on the front street in Staindrop, some with bay windows, towards the end of the 1800s. He entered into partnership with William John Lord, a joiner by profession, of Church View, Ferryhill. They had it in mind to buy land and build houses in Chilton, an up-and-coming place around 1910. With a shortage of houses for miners working at the two collieries, there was plenty of scope for a builder with streets and shops going up, from Eden Terrace to Arthur Street.

In 1911 they were successful in purchasing a piece of land from Sir William Eden, the landlord, situated adjacent to the Great North Road where Durham Road now stands, for less than £500.

On instruction from Sir William's solicitors, Parkin and Lord agreed to the following: "That no dwelling house or building erected or to be erected thereon would be used as a Workmen's Club or as and for an Inn, Beer House, Tavern or house or place for the sale of intoxicating liquors or for the purpose of carrying on any noisesome or offensive trade or business AND that no dog or dogs shall be kept on the said pieces or parcels of land hereby conveyed or in the dwelling houses or other buildings or erections to be erected or erected thereon".

Parkin and Lord were eventually successful in the purchase of land from Lord Eldon, who owned roughly the northern half of Chilton Buildings. This piece of land was enough to build half of Eden Terrace. It would seem that whilst Parkin and Lord were building their half of Eden Terrace, the other half was being erected by someone else. Houses may have been given a number, and let as they were completed. It appears that the builders were working from each end towards the middle of the terrace and may not have consulted with each other. When the terrace was joined, there was no space for number 19. It remains the same to this day in Eden Terrace.

Margaret Sowerby (nee Parkin) lives in Durham Road in one of the houses built by her grandfather. I am indebted to her for some of this information and the accompanying drawing and signature page of the conveyance of 1911, which includes Sir William's signature.

The following extract, from the Rural Council records dated 11th February 1909, states, "owing to the large and ever increasing population in the Townships of Ferryhill and Chilton, the time has come for the division of the Township into Wards. That for the Township of Chilton, the two existing polling districts be formed into separate Wards. One of such districts, comprising Dene Bridge Row, Chilton Buildings and Windlestone Rows."

This area was to have two councillors and thus had an increased influence on the local council activities.

From 1900 to 1910, there was a sudden and dramatic growth of the village and there developed a community of people with one common interest: the mines.

The houses built in Chilton and Windlestone were similar to those in South View, minus the "T" fall in the back bedroom, a typical working-class dwelling, to be found in most of the mining villages in the Durham Coalfield. Usually two rooms down and two/three bedrooms, with the earth closet over the back yard, next to the coal house.

Eden Terrace

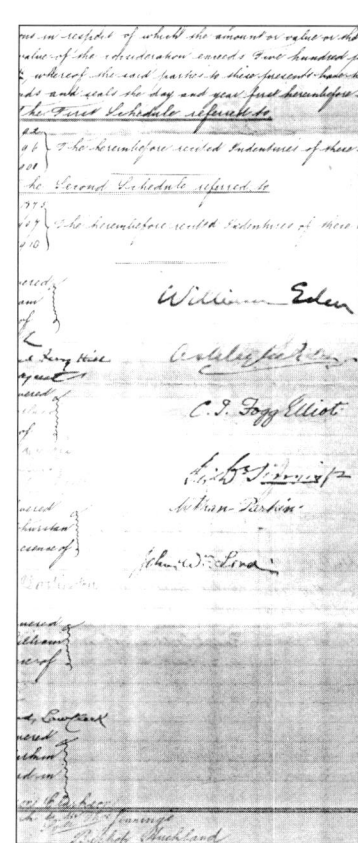

Document showing William Eden's signature

Growing Pains

The monumental increase in the population was raised at council meetings. It was decided that more houses were urgently needed. There had been a long period of stability at Chilton Pit and both communities were still growing.

At this present time, in 1916, there were 75 workmen walking three to five miles to their work at Chilton Colliery. The 45 houses suggested were inadequate; the figure of 100 houses was thought to be more realistic and they should be built as soon as possible.

West Chilton Terrace built for H. Stobart & Co in 1905

Local transport became an important issue. The Railway Company was asked to build a railway station at Chilton, but they declined. However, the Council was not to be deterred in their efforts and contacted several bus companies, with a view to having a service from Ferryhill to Ferryhill Station and on to Chilton Buildings.

Generally, bus services and communications improved; the two communities of Chilton and

Clare Lodge, set in extensive gardens, on the bank between Rushyford and Chilton. Built about 1910 for Dr. Sheedy who carried on his surgery from the house. In the coal era it was home to successive colliery managers at Mainsforth Pit.

Windlestone were beginning to have an influence,with the surrounding villages, as they matured. The reopening of Chilton Pit in 1902 was, without doubt, the major reason for the expansion of the two communities. Even so, Windlestone in 1906 experienced a very similar boom with their share of growing realised in Prospect Terrace, Arthur and Albert Streets.

Although the locals were proud of their own patch, it became increasingly obvious that Chilton and Windlestone were now completely integrated. Represented by one council, their future success would depend on all residents pulling together for the common good of Chilton Buildings.

*A group of smart, young Chilton folks. Given the chance on any occasion, the women never let their menfolk down. Harry Hall **(ctr.)**, with the baby and my old informant Ernie Hope **5th left.***

The Women

Progress revolved around the decisions men made, with hardly a mention of the womenfolk, and yet without their unstinting support the men would have got nowhere, a fact commonly accepted by everyone in the community. Life for the women of the household had always been hard,with little or no recognition in public. They had very little free time, with only a small number working in industry. The families were large and looking after the house was a full-time occupation.

The mother, or her children, never had the opportunity to leave the neighbourhood. With family planning a thing of the future, the female vitality was sapped by frequent pregnancies.

The average age for marriages was males 25 and women 23. The reason for this, probably, was the difficulty in getting a house. Miners at this time were given a rent allowance of 4 pence a shift (old money) from the mine owners and had to find their own accommodation. Since most of the buildings were completed by 1914, it became increasingly difficult for miners to get a house. Add to this the other financial problems of marriage, it is not surprising that the marriage rate was low.

CHAPTER FIVE

Sport and Recreation

Sport and Recreation

They were probably playing football here as soon as there were enough men or boys to put a team together. Many names come to mind: of those who were involved and spent much of their time and devotion playing and running football clubs in the village. The late Joe Mellville must rank as one of those. His playing days spanned the 1940s and 50s and afterwards he spent many years running various Chilton teams.

Amateur football was well supported in the mining villages of South West Durham, Chilton being no exception. The young men who are playing for Chilton now as we approach the millennium know what a great feeling it is to succeed in the cups and league matches. They will appreciate what it must have been like for those playing for Chilton Colliery Recreation AFC in what became the greatest era of football the village was ever to witness, during the 1920s.

Preceding the Chilton Rec. AFC exploits, West Chilton AFC were playing in the Ferryhill District League, Division 1 in 1914. Their headquarters being the Colliery Institute in West Chilton Terrace, provided by the colliery's owners, Henry Stobart. The field they played on, was provided by G. E. Young of West Chilton Farm. Mr. Young was a patron of the football club alongside most of the influential people in the village and surrounding area.

The Colliery Institute, 80/81 West Chilton Terrace, provided a reading room with tables and benches. Daily papers, periodicals and a library were there for the members' use. The storeroom contained footballs and other games equipment, such as quoits, bats, balls, etc.

The Colliery Institute
80/81 West Chilton Terrace

This West Chilton AFC Season 1914-15 membership card gives one an indication of the people involved, with some of the more prominent patrons identified by their status or occupation quite easily. Of the remainder, however, one might find the following list interesting.

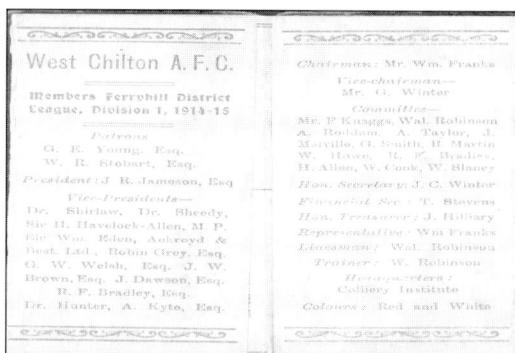

J. R. Jameson Undermanager (Chilton Colliery); Jack Hillary, 1 Oswald Terr, (Miners financial Sec.); G. Winter, Dene Bridge Row, Miner; J. C. Winter, Dene Bridge Row, Miner; T. Steven, West Chilton Terr, Miner. The committee were miners working at Chilton or Windlestone.

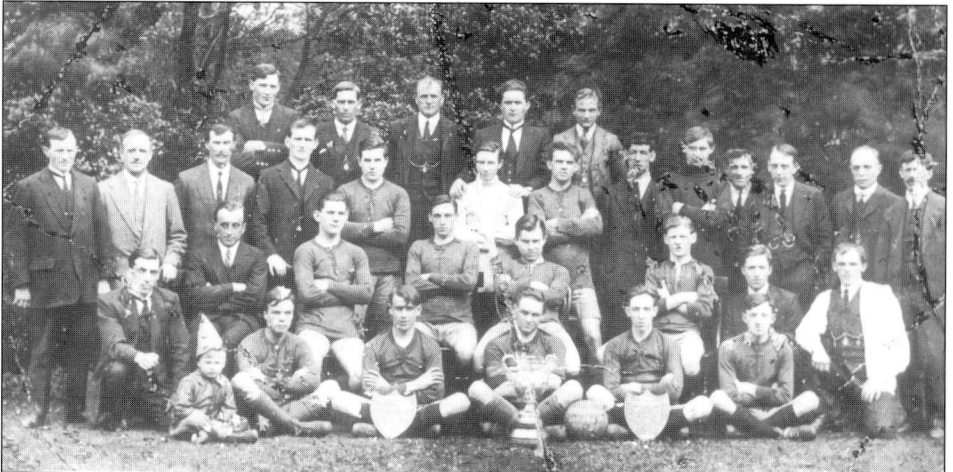

Windlestone Juniors

Players: Back Row standing: *Bob Wilson (L.B.) W. Wilson (G) A. Bradshaw (R.B.)* **Sitting:** *R. Hope (L.H.) C. Lofthouse (C.H.) Lowe (R.H.) R. Latheron (Res.)* **Front Row :** *J. Martin (O.L.) S. Winter (I.L.) P. Longstaff (C.F.) S. Wilson (I.R.) A. Oughton (O.R.)* **Trainer :** *T. Wilson.*

Our old detective, Ernie Hope, identified these young lads in 1979, when he was 83. It had been a good season, winning the Durham Junior Cup beating Tanfield Lea in a replay and beaten finalists in the Eden Junior Cup. S.Winter (Sam) in later life was one of a small group in Chilton who possessed a horse and cart, a common enough sight until the 1960s. He was often seen, his cart stacked up with furniture, helping people move house from one part of the village to another. He was a member of St. Aidan's Church Choir most of his life and, with a fine tenor voice, was ever present until he was unable to attend through ill health during the 1980s.

Chilton School Team 1911 including 1 International and 4 County players.

Extreme left, *Sam Raynor (headmaster).* **Top left,** *H. R. Chittenden (teacher).* **Centre,** *wearing his International Cap, Sam Hartnell.* **Behind him**, *Jimmy Yare* **to his left***, Joe Lamb,* **to the right,** *Alf Martin* **(both standing)**. *Ernie Hope is extreme right sitting with W. Shield (staff). Staff members,* **top right** *J.Bates and J.Connors.*

Sam Hartnell, Schoolboy International

Sam Hartnell lived in Chilton, and he attended and played for Chilton Council School in the first season after it was built in 1909. Playing in the Spennymoor Schools' League, he was picked to play for England during the 1910/11 season after some good performances in the County side. His exploits caught the attention of the whole village.

For the record, he came to prominence in 1909/10 when his team won the Spennymoor Schools' League and the Markham Cup. He went on to captain the Inter-League Team, winning the Teesside Challenge Shield and a Wear Valley Shield medal.

In the 1910/11 season Hartnell was picked to play at "inside right" for England against Scotland at St. James' Park, Newcastle. Playing "centre forward" for Durham against Northumberland and "full back" in a return match was a measure of his versatility. In all, he scored 86 goals in the process.

Sam must have been on cloud nine, doing what most schoolboys only get to dream about. It did not finish there. For his outstanding performance he received a medal from the residents of Chilton, as a mark of appreciation for being the first International Schoolboy from Chilton.

Memorial Cottages, Main Street, Chilton. Built by Henry Stobart and Co in memory of those who gave their lives during the Great War 1914-18.

Dave Wallace, headmaster at Chilton Junior School, raised a question, "Did he go on to play professionally?" After making some enquiries, it seems that Sam joined the Army during the First World War and was killed. It appears that a brilliant talent and life was, sadly, cut short. Incidentally, on the Roll of Honour plaque on the Memorial Cottages in the main street, there is the name S. Hartnell inscribed. If one visits Kirk Merrington churchyard, to the rear, you will find his memorial stone.

Chilton Colliery Recreation Association Club

The title of this section is quite a mouthful so I will refer to this team as Chilton Colly RA, for our journey through some of their exploits during the 1920s.

Whilst the 1920s saw more downs than ups on the jobs front and most families were finding it hard to make ends meet, there was one topic of conversation guaranteed to bring a smile to many a carewarn face. One forgot his or her troubles, at least for a while, when the subject got round to Chilton Colly RA, who, through the 1920s, did their fair share to lift the gloom which sometimes descended on the village like a black cloud from time to time.

It is more than likely that Chilton Colly RA was formed from two local teams, playing prior to the 1920s. Dene Bridge Seniors played in the Mid-Durham and Ferryhill Leagues and won the Ferryhill District League in 1920. West Chilton AFC were members of the Ferryhill District League, with their headquarters being the Chilton Colly. Institute in West Chilton Terrace.

Chilton Colliery RA, was formed in 1921, and in the main, it was made up of people associated with the pit. None more so than Mr. Durno, the colliery undermanager. His influence and commitment to the team was such, he ensured that all those playing for the team who had jobs at the pit, and that was almost everyone were available when there was a match on. Mr. Durno's dedication and enthusiasm was an example to the others, the patrons, club officers and so on, down to the turnstile men at the entry gates of the field. For those who were involved, their first priority, in their spare time was the football club, the team and the results they got.

The team had an army of helpers, the supporters, with one thing in mind - the success of the club. The women washed the soiled football strips out, boiling them in the *set pot, and possing them in the *poss tub, having their reward when the team trotted onto the field on match days in their red and whites with black shorts.

Set pot, made of cast iron, set into brickwork over a coal fire in the kitchen, used for boiling white clothes.
Poss tub, a wooden barrel, similar to the old beer barrel, filled with hot, soapy water for washing coloureds using a poss stick. Made of wood with a handle at one end with a wider cylindrical piece at the other and used for pushing the clothes through the water (possing).

Chilton joined the Palatine League in 1921/22, but the tracing of our team's exploits begins, for us with the 1922/23 season. Their football ground was aptly named "The Pit Field", situated behind Dene Bridge Row, at the top end. It was two fields over, access being gained through a gate opposite numbers 23/24 and along a path over the first field. The football stand and changing rooms were at the far end of the field, next to the pit heaps.

Chilton Colliery RA 1922
2nd l: *Mr. Durno (Chairman) next Ric Pearson,* **7th l:** *Bradshaw,* **sitting, 2nd l:** *Thompson, then Catterick, Martin and Winter*

Palatine League 1922/23

This was their second season. The team was starting to take shape and names like Catterick, Martin, Winter and Thompson were to appear regularly in the seasons to come.

At this stage, there was one thing that no one, the team or the staff, could have forseen - that they, as amateurs, were on the brink of a run of success which was to last five seasons and was to make Chilton Colly RA a team to be feared and respected by the top amateur and, to some extent, professional teams of the day.

The team playing during the middle of this season is as follows: Gowland, Martin, Mould, Catterick, York, Thompson, Lamb, Coyle, Gent, Robinson, Pearson

This 11 played Sunderland in the third round of the Durham Senior Cup and were beaten 4-0. Qualifying this far had been a good effort, and having Sunderland at home made it a great day for the fans and the team, even though they were the losers. They competed in five cup campaigns and won the Palatine Charity Cup and ended the season in second position.

The following are the cup stages they achieved:

Wingate Charity Cup - *1st. Round*, Durham Senior Cup - *3rd Round Proper*,

F.A. Amateur Cup - *3rd Qualifying Round*, Durham Hospital Cup - *Semi Final*

Thompson was the leading scorer with 17 league goals, Martin on 13, Gent 8 and Winter 5. In the Cups, A. Robinson 8, H. Catterick 7 and Bowes 6.

Those teams opposing Chilton in the Palatine League were as follows: Hetton United, Ferryhill Athletic, Shildon Railway, Trimdon Grange, Coundon United, West Stanley Rovers, Thornley Albion, Wheatley Hill Colliery, Chester-le-Street Res. and Spennymoor Res.

Coxhoe Pottery, Stillington St. John, Darlington RA and Dunston Atlas Villa were some of the teams met with in the cup competitions.

In these times, with no television and little in the way of radio (wireless sets as they were called), the football team in most of the villages was one of the main focal points. As such, they used to attract good crowds, often many hundreds, and, at big matches, into the thousands. It seems almost impossible judging by today's attendances; never-the-less, it was true. So it was then and still is now, no sooner has one season ended before the next one appears to be upon us. As always, when the new season beckons, everyone is hopeful that they will do well and win something. The excitement of the unknown and the unexpected in football is always there to whet the appetite.

Chilton's 1923/24 season would open in such a way. They were still playing on the Pit Field behind Dene Bridge Row. The fact that they started the season £15 in debt and finished with a profit of £209 speaks volumes, as you will see from the paper cutting opposite.

The performance table shown illustrates the effort and stamina required to succeed, playing 58 games in a season, twelve of those in sixteen days. This clipping makes impressive reading, even to this day one feels proud of their achievements. Winning four cups and reaching the semi-final of the F.A. Amateur Cup, would be a talking point for many years thereafter.

The handbill on page 85 highlights Chilton's interest in the 4th round of the Amateur Cup against Dulwich Hamlet, beating them 3-0 and eventually going out 3-0 to Clapton in the semi final at Darlington in front of a crowd of 14,068.

And what about going to the Star Picture Hall after the team had won. In those days, it was a silent movie with someone at the front of the hall playing music on the piano to suit the mood of the picture. Make no mistake, it was every bit as exciting to the audience then as it is now with our present-day movie blockbusters.

As the season progressed, another player, W. Bowran, became ever-present in the Chilton side. In his first season with the club he scored 36 league and cup goals. He was to stay with Chilton for many years and seldom lost his scoring touch. However, he was not on his own. Thompson scored 25 goals, Reed 22 and A. Winter 18.

The Palatine League 1924/25

For Chilton Colly RA the new football season could not come quick enough for some, with a new ground and stand beckoning, although not quite finished when the season began. Many would naturally wonder if they could carry on where they left off in 1923/4. Being realistic, they were starting from scratch again, like every other team in the league. They would have to play well and have some luck if they were to get anywhere.

The "red letter" day, the opening day for the new ground was 26th November 1924. To mark the occasion they played Middlesbrough Reserves. Chilton won 4-3, the teams were as follows:

Chilton RA - Guthrie, Draper, Hodgson, Lamb, Catterick, Taylor, Winter, Thompson (3) Bowran, Robinson, Scurr (1).

Middlesbro Res. - Gowland, Wilson, French, Murray, Blake, Ashman, Dickenson (1), Dickson (1), Hick (1), Cochrane, J. T. Williams.

Chilton RA were entered into five cup competitions.Their winning ways continued as the following details will testify.

Durham Hospital Cup	Winners	beat Trimdon Grange
National Orphanage Cup	Winners	beat Trimdon Grange
Durham Senior Cup	Finalists	lost to Sunderland Res.
F.A. Cup	5th Qual. Rd.	lost to Crook 3-4
F.A. Am. Cup	4th Rd. Proper	lost to Northern Nomads

Chilton could count themselves very unlucky not to land the Durham Senior Cup, after drawing 1-1 with Sunderland Res. at Bishop Auckland in front of 8,000 spectators, with Taylor missing a penalty four minutes from time. In the replay at Darlington, Chilton lost 1-0.They went on to win the league and appeared to be on a rollercoaster, their impressive form of the previous season being maintained. They scored a record number of goals in the cup competitions in this season.

Played	Won	Drawn	Lost	For	Against	Pts.
29	22	4	3	86	32	

In the league

16	15	1	0	24	12	31

Bowran was again top scorer with 37 league and cup goals, followed by Thompson 28 and Robinson 21. This was an excellent follow-up of the previous season, with plenty to smile about at the next Annual General Meeting.

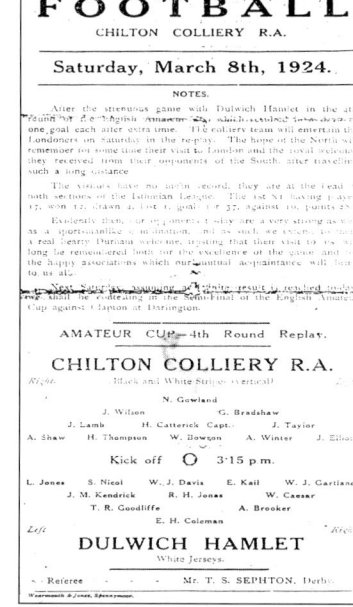

The meeting of Chilton Colliery R. A. and Sunderland Res. in the final of the Durham Challenge Cup created tremendous interest, and when the game commenced on the Bishop Auckland ground to-day there was a crowd of 8,000.

Sunderland won the toss, and Chilton were soon attacking. Scurr made a sparkling run on the left, but was dispossessed by Lodge. Death went away on the Sunderland right and was making for goal when he was fouled by Hodgson just outside the penalty area. The kick was nicely placed by Coxford, but Hodgson cleared well under pressure.

Chilton afterwards made one or two clever moves but they generally found the Sunderland halves too good for them. Rogers set Fryer away on the Sunderland right, but the winger's centre was smothered by Taylor at the expense of a fruitless corner.

A minute later Fryer forced Taylor to concede a corner, but Death was dispossessed whilst working for an opening. Owens cleared with a long kick which sent Bowran and Scurr away, but the latter's shot was just wide of the post.

Sunderland again got away, and Ranson presented HOGG with a fine opening. Hogg's first shot struck the post, but he recovered possession and beat Guthrie with a fine shot, sending the ball into the corner of the net.

Following this reverse Chilton made greater efforts, and the Sunderland goal had a narrow escape when Bowran was dispossessed when about to shoot from close range.

The Colliers were now finding their form and enjoyed quite as much of the play as their opponents.

Young was fortunate to clear when Bowran had made a determined effort. The back appeared to handle when clearing, but claims for a penalty were ignored.

Shortly afterwards Robinson secured possession close in, and his final shot caused Stoneham to dive full length to save.

A quick movement by Sunderland saw Hogg create an opening for Death, but the latter shot wide.

Chilton became very persistent towards the interval, and gave the Sunderland defence a warm time. Stoneham was called upon to save in quick succession from Lamb and Taylor.

Death was fouled on several occasions when making tracks for goal, and there were some exciting moments in the Chilton goal. At the other end Stoneham had to throw out under difficult circumstances, and the interval came with Chilton applying strong pressure. Half-time:—

Sunderland Reserves 1
Chilton Colliery 0

Chilton opened the second half with a promising attack on the left, and Scurr had an exciting duel with Ditchburn, the latter eventually clearing. The Colliers attacked repeatedly.

Then Sunderland broke away, a narrow escape when Stoneham saved the foot of the post from Scurr, who was the most prominent player in the Chilton front rank.

The Colliers kept up the pressure, but poor shooting nullified good approach work. After 30 minutes' play Scurr sent across a fine centre for THOMPSON to head the equalising goal amid great excitement.

Taylor missed a penalty for Chilton four minutes from time. Result:—

SUNDERLAND RES. 1
CHILTON COLLIERY 1

Chilton Colliery RAFC before their match with Sunderland Res. at Bishop Auckland, 11th. April 1925.
None players, *l-r: Charlie Wayman (treasurer), Ric Pearson, Jo Murphy (trainer), G.Lamp, E.Attwood,*
Players: back row, l-r: *Lamb, Taylor, A. Martin, Guthrie, H. Owens, H. Hodgson.*
Sitting: l-r: *Thompson, A. Winter, H. Catterick (capt.), A. Robinson, Scurr.*

N.B. The Durham Senior Cup, referred to previously, is the Durham Challenge Cup, the top amateur competition in the county.

Paper cuttings are not unlike books; a good narrative or report can easily transport a person to that time. I have found this to be true on reading some of them and imagining being on the terraces, watching these games. They were played over 70 years ago, and yet it seems as though it was only yesterday. Fortunately, there are a number of these cuttings in this book, the first of them, "Durham Challenge Cup" dated 11 April 1925 that one may enjoy reading, as I have.

To complete the 1924/5 season, a copy of the membership card on page 87, may be of interest. It is no surprise to see Sir A. F. Pease, Baronet, as the club president, with Stobart now only a partner. Mr. Kellett was then colliery manager at Chilton, and John Herriotts former MP., he took office again in 1929. H. T. Barker (Harry) owned the grocer's shop at the end of Eden Terrace, opposite St. Aidan's Church. Alf Jaques had West Chilton Farm, adjacent to the football field and a butcher's shop, 2 Eden Terrace. Tom Pickering was the local barber, 7 Eden Terrace. F. T. Richardson had the chemist's shop, 1 Durham Road. Dr. Mathew Hunter is one of the older patrons, he was with West Chilton AFC back in 1914. Many of those mentioned and, others who appear on the card, were known to me when I was a boy growing up in Windlestone.

Times were good for the moment, but would it last? Everything depended on how the pits were going. The people of Chilton and Windlestone did not need a crystal ball, they would take things as they came; it was probably the only way.

The Northern Alliance League 1925/26

There were few people in work, another recession and the 1926 National Strike just around the corner. Not a lot to smile about at this time but the football team was doing its best to raise everyone's morale. With many out of work there was plenty of time to train for matches.

Chilton RA's exploits had, so far, done much to lift the gloom. They had applied to join the Northern Alliance and were accepted. Geographically, they were by far the most southerly club in the league. Their nearest rivals being Craghead, Birtley and Consett, two of the longest travels would be Mickley near Prudhoe and Ashington. Strange teams and grounds would be another test for our heroes, with the season more anticipated than ever.

Chilton, now with a brand new ground and stand, to say nothing of the army of officials and supporters to spur them on, would be trying their utmost to get off to a good start.

Once again, Chilton was in the thick of cup competitions. In the FA Cup they had a tremendous run, reaching the 3rd round proper, Carlisle were their first round victims, beating them away from home 2-0. They became an English league side three years later.

Rochdale, who were in the old League Division 3 North, came to Chilton, in the 2nd round and were held to a 1-1 draw in front of 5,000 spectators. A cutting here gives a report on this match.

Chilton travelled to Rochdale on 17th December 1925 and beat them 2-1. This was no mean feat, when one considers that Rochdale were third from the top of the league at the end of the season.

In the 3rd round Chilton were drawn against South Shields away. At this time South Shields, who were later to become Gateshead in 1930, were playing in the 2nd Division of the English League, against the likes of Middlesbrough, Wolves and Derby County, to name but a few. It would be a tough match for our amateurs, indeed it was, losing 3-0 to professionals. Beaten but not disgraced, with a match report here for the interested reader.

In the other cup competitions, they were very unlucky to be drawn away in three semi-finals and on each occasion, lost by the odd goal. They were as follows:

Northern Alliance Cup - lost to Consett 0-1

Durham Senior Cup - lost to Bp. Auckland 2-3

National Orphanage Cup - lost to Stockton 1-2

Chilton Colliery RA membership card season 1924-25

It would be unfair not to mention the excitement that was probably created when Chilton beat Sunderland Res. in the 3rd round of the Senior Cup at Chilton, in front of a crowd of 3,000. In that semi-final with Bishop Auckland, the match was played in front of 6.879 spectators, paying £189.2.9d.

They say success breeds success. It was certainly true for Chilton, who continued with their "purple patch" (glory days). They became Northern Alliance Champions at the first attempt.

The Northern Alliance 1926/27

The season found our footballers playing in their second season in the Northern Alliance. They were without their brilliant centre-half and inspirational captain, Harry Catterick, who went to Stockport for a number of seasons. Later on he went into management. In 1959 he was the manager of Rochdale who were in Division 3 of the Football League. His name was also linked to Everton and Sheffield Wednesday.

Out of the many supporters Chilton had, our own Tommy Buckle would have been hard to beat. The records he kept of the team's exploits have enabled me to follow their progress in detail. Chilton RA had come a long way in a short time, the sweet smell of success dimming the memories of those not-so-far-off days when some of the players were part of the Dene Bridge Seniors team. This season, Chilton finished a creditable fourth in the league. In the cups they reached the FA Cup 2nd round beaten by Accrington Stanley 3-0 and the Nat. Homes Cup final, beaten by Willington after two replays. So the ambitious pot was still on the boil at the end of the season.

To The End of a Great 5 Years - The Northern League 1927/28

Chilton, off their past record, applied to join the Northern League, in the hope that they might be accepted. They had beaten many of the teams in this league on previous occasions during the last four seasons and on the basis of this must have thought they stood a chance.
As it happened, they were admitted and would be playing some of the best amateur teams in the region.

Chilton Officials and the team would have to "dig in" and work hard like never before and hope "Lady Luck" stayed with them. The good times had in such a short history were to their credit, but they were now amongst the big boys. This was something every committee man, player and supporter had strived for. Chilton RA had arrived, it was up to them to show the rest of the League what they could do.

In their first three games they played away to South Bank, Stockton and Crook. They were beaten each time, a poor start.

The next five games found them winning three and drawing two, the opposition being Ferryhill Athletic, Crook, Cockfield and Stanley, twice. A big improvement. In the following game they played Bishop Auckland at Kingsway and were beaten 4-3.

What happened next was like something one would read in a children's fairy story book.

They won the next ten games on the trot!
Tow Law 5-2 A.: Ferryhill Ath.5-0 H.: Bp.Auckland 4-1 H.:
Esh Winning 4-0 A.: Cockfield 4-1 H.: Tow Law 4-2 H,:
Willington 2-0 H.: Loftus Alb. 2-1 A.: Willington 2-1 A.:
South Bank 2-1 H.:

To follow this remarkable run, Chilton played a draw at Langley Park 1-1. Judging by the previous ten games, they were probably due for a draw or a defeat, but there was no way of stopping the Chilton Rollercoaster.

Chilton won the following five games. Langley Park 5-0 H.: Whitby 7-2 H.: Esh Winning 5-3 H.: Loftus Alb. 2-1 H.: Stockton 3-1 H. The sixth match, at Whitby, was a 1-1 draw.

With this kind of form, Chilton were going to be up there with the rest of them and in with a good chance of winning something - and they did. Chilton RA won the Northern League Championship at the first attempt. This was indeed their "Crowning Glory" and a fitting end to a remarkable run of five seasons. It must have been great cause for celebration for the players, officials and supporters. The culmination of five years of dedication had placed the young village of Chilton on the map in a way which was not likely to be repeated again.

During this period, there were four players ever present, apart from the odd injury: Winter, Bowran, Robinson and Martin. Many others, such as Catterick, Thompson, Hodgson, Pretty and Gregg, to name but a few, should not be forgotten, as they all contributed to the overall success of the team.

This is the team who played Stockton in the last game of the season, beating them 3-1 at home: Spence, Willis, Jones, Pretty, Bowran, Denham, Martin, Winter, Palmer, Robinson, Harle.

Their League Record:

Played	Won	Lost	Drawn	For	Against	Pts.
24	16	3	5	75	35	37

In the cup competitions they were beaten finalists in the Northern League Challenge Cup, losing to Willington 3-2 after extra time in a replay.

Shortly afterwards from a pass by Parker, Trotter was bearing down on the Chilton goal, when Guthrie ran out and cleared smartly.

Despite the heavy ground, the pace was hot.

Smith was conspicuous with a couple of shots, the first being cleared by one of the backs, and the second going over the bar.

Thirlaway narrowly missed with a left foot shot, and Trotter also had hard lines with a good drive.

At this period, the Seasiders were dominating the game and the Chilton defence, though stubborn, was very severely tested. Some good passing was done by the home forwards and halves, but the ball was sticky and somewhat difficult to control.

Hutchinson headed wide from a corner by Trotter. Parker next ran up and centred to Trotter, who shot, but Guthrie saved at the expense of a corner. Smith then tried a shot, but went wide of the mark. Half-time.—
South Shields 1
Chilton Colliery 0

South Shields opened the second half in aggressive style, and from a centre by Thirlaway Wilson headed past.

Taylor led the Chilton forwards in a counter-attack, and Ridley had to concede a corner, which was fruitless.

The Shields right flank was conspicuous in a further attack. Thirlaway, with a good opportunity, made a bad miss, and Wilson also shot wide.

The Seasiers kept up continuous pressure, but were unable to penetrate, their forwards' work at close quartes leaving a lot to be desired.

Owens and Hodgson were kept busy, and defended so well that Guthrie in goal did not have a great deal to do, though once he cleared well from Thirlaway.

At this period Chilton were forced to concentrate on defence, and little was seen of their forwards.

Further success came the Shields way after 25 minutes in the second half, when the ball after being fisted out by Guthrie from Trotter, went to WILSON who, with a first time left foot drive, left the goalkeeper helpless.

After half an hour PARKER scored a third from Thirlaway's centre. Result:—
SOUTH SHIELDS 3
CHILTON COLLIERY 0

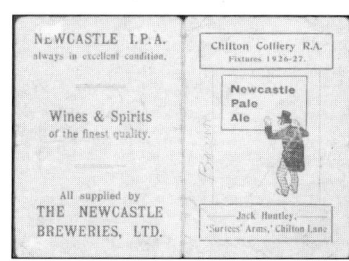

*Chilton Colliery RA fixtures card
1926/27*

Charlie Wayman in his Newcastle United strip about 1946.

Chilton Colly. Welfare Ground, scene of many triumphs over the years

There has been success for many future teams bearing the name of Chilton and there still is, but as time has shown, none to exceed the exploits and the big crowds of the 1920s.

The players were the community's heroes, but there were many unsung heroes, such as Mr. W.Durno (chairman), *Charlie Wayman (treasurer), W. Pickering (financial sec.), members of the Committee, the trainers, those women who washed and ironed the players' strips every week (red and white striped shirts and black shorts), the volunteers who looked after the pitch, and not least "The Supporters".

Charlie Wayman

Wayman transferred to Southampton in 1947 for a record £10,000. His transfer to Preston North End in 1950 was one of their most notable acquisitions up to that date in Division 1. In 1952/3 he became the clubs top scorer with 24 goals.

Wayman achieved a record by scoring in every round of the FA Cup, including the Cup Final, playing West Bromwich in 1954, losing 3-1. He also played for Middlesbrough and Darlington.

* Charlie Wayman senior whose son Charlie's footballing exploits are noted here

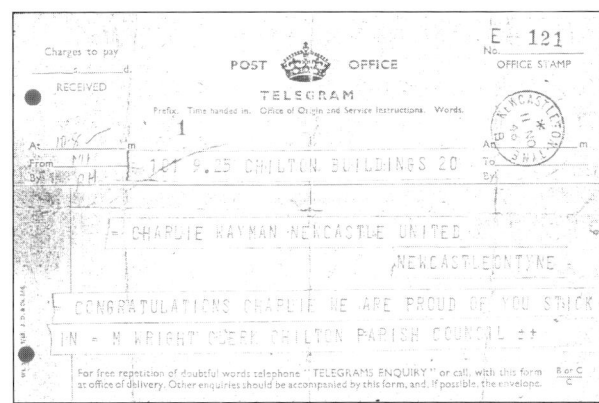

A telegram showing how proud Chilton were of the success of one of their sons.

Chilton School Team 1931 ***back row l to r:*** *G. Foster, A. Philips, R. Smedley, W. G. Waite, (staff) R. Ashpool, H. Sullivan, T. Wilson* ***sitting:*** *W. Mathews, A. B. Ross (head), T. Langdale (capt), J. Nattrass (Staff), G. Gowland,* ***front:*** *A. Wilson, M. Oliver (shown in greater detail on page 101)*

Charlie Wayman, ***centre front****, during his time at Preston North End and sitting alongside the legendary England International Tom Finney,* ***sitting first on the left.***

Chilton Athletic 1944/45 ***back row, players only l to r:*** *J. Dunn, G. Wilkinson, J. Mellville* ***middle:*** *A. Porter, W. Lamb, W. Matthews, J. Fisher* ***front:*** *J. Yates, M. Oliver, F. Fisher, F. Brabbon, K. Robinson*

Billy Matthews and his bride, late 1940s. Billy was a good bat. I remember him hitting one ball straight over West Chilton Terrace for six. He played football for Chilton Athletic at this time. He worked at Chilton Pit as a Deputy, living in Dene Bridge Row most of his life; he still lives in the village. Guard of honour, **left side first:** *Jack Cheesmond, Bob Morton, Tom Oyston.* **Right side:** *?, Alan Leighton, Sam Robinson. Page, Barry Matthews*

(shown in greater detail on page 101)

Cricket in Chilton

The cricket ground, next to the football ground, opened in 1924. Teams playing there achieved very little during the first few years.

Billy Lamb, a former resident now living in Ferryhill, used to be a keen footballer and cricketer for Chilton. Like many of his colleagues, he worked at Chilton Pit, and was an under official for a number of years until the pit closed. He became involved with cricket in 1935 with the team playing in the Mid-Durham League. "It was run by Jimmy Simpson with players like Bill Fairy, Graham White and Harry Howe, who had only one arm and managed to bowl very well and also use the bat to good effect. I, as a schoolboy became the scorer. By the war years everything came to a standstill.

The local lads at the pit started to take an interest, and practised and eventually formed a team. Transport was difficult and we travelled to away matches on bikes, with bat and pads strapped to the crossbars.

Getting the field cut was a problem, but we got a set of horse-drawn Gang Mowers from the Eden Estate at Windlestone Hall, and the only thing we required then was a horse. This was supplied by W. S. Shield at Chilton Farm down the Station Road. Volunteers biked down for the horse, left the bike and led the horse up to the ground, and vice versa to take the horse back to the stable. This was done many times during the season. We were very grateful to Billy Shield who played cricket for Durham City and Northumberland.

We formed a club with Sammy Robinson (treasurer), Cecil Leighton, Tommy Hartnell, George Smith (schoolteacher), Tommy Oyston and quite a few more on the committee, with myself as secretary. We played all friendly games, Ringtons Tea at Newcastle, to which we travelled each time by train from Ferryhill Station. Other matches were arranged, including Dean Bank and Mainsforth. After the war, we joined the South West Durham League, which consisted of many works teams from Darlington. We won this league in 1946 and 1952 and the Harrison Shield in 1954. After this time, interest waned and players moved away and the happy times all came to an end". G. W. Lamb 1999

Chilton Colliery Cricket Club, members of the South West Durham League and winners in 1946
standing l tor: *George Smith, Sam Robinson, Tom Oyston, Billy Lamb, ?, Bob Smedley, Bob Elliot, Alan Leighton, Tom Hartnell, Cecil Leighton*
sitting: *Jack Cheesmond, Jack Pearson, Harry Greener, ?, Stan Leighton*

Leisure Time

Chilton Institute housed a billiard/snooker table upstairs, where a game cost two pence (old money); the loser paid. There was a room for cards, chess, dominoes and draughts. A changing room for the football team was another feature. The Recreation Association also prepared swimming facilities at the mines reservoir; diving boards were erected and a rota of lifeguards was organised by the miners.

Situated next to the Council School, opposite Dene Terrace, stood the Victory Club, sometimes called the Comrades Club. One can only assume it was built after about 1919 following victory in the First World War. There were dances on a weekly basis, a violin and an accordion providing the music. This became very popular for the locals as well as attracting people from the surrounding villages.

Concerts were held in Windlestone Institute hall quite often; people provided their own entertainment, staging talent competitions for small prizes.

Voucher book to commemorate the Jubilee of the club

Chilton and Windlestone Workingmen's Club

"The Club", in its first premises Charlotte Terrace, about 1913, not far from the Board School, with the railway crossing in between.

The Club's full title is quite a mouthful. However, the important contribution the Club has made to the social life of the community cannot be overstated. To those in the early part of the century who were members of Temperance Societies, and there were many, together with those with strong religious beliefs against the sale of intoxicating liquor, it is small wonder that establishments such as the Club ever got off the ground.

Chilton and Windlestone Club today

Chilton and Windlestone Club with the club steward's living quarters on the first floor. To the rear of the club is a large, excellent concert hall/functions room. All in all, a big club, with a reputation at times of having some of the big names in show business appear on the stage.

A concert programme from 1914

In 1909, on Sunday 23rd May, the Workingmen's Club was founded by a public meeting held in secret, as it were, ensuring that it did not come to the notice of Sir William Eden, the landowner. The meeting, held in a quarry at the side of the Great North Road, now the A167, was attended by only ten miners. It was a well-known fact that Sir William was against most ventures of this type. The premises, although quite small considering the initial membership was 125, boasted a large bar downstairs and a committee and billiard room upstairs.

Its takings in 1909 were £18 per week; this amounted to a lot of money in view of the fact that they had a well-established rival in the Encombe Inn, now the Wheatsheaf.

Support for the Club was strong and membership grew, making it a permanent feature. The Club remained in these premises until 1937, when the new Club was completed on the site they occupy to this day. It would be a "red letter day", no doubt. With this new building, Chilton and Windlestone Club became one of the premier clubs in South

Chilton Concert party
*Ernie Hope in the 1920s **sitting 3rd left.** he is identified like no other, appearing in this book through the course of his life.*

West Durham. Well-run and efficient, with a reputation for looking after its members, young and old.

Aged members and their wives could enjoy at Christmas a first-class treat, usually on a Saturday, which included a meal, presents and free raffles in the afternoon, followed in the evening by first-class entertainment all on a grand scale. Children and parents were given a trip out in the summer to a local seaside town, Redcar and South Shields being two of the more popular places visited. The trip was free, with each child receiving pocket money, sweets and fruit. It was a big undertaking for the club management and committee, who acted as stewards on the day to ensure all went well. For many years, the number of buses hired in could exceed fifty. Deckchairs and folding beach tents, whilst in plentiful supply on a normal day, were quickly snapped up when the trip came in. Where there had been an empty beach at 9.30 am, it was a sea of humanity by 10.00 am. The funding for these occasions came from all manner of functions, with a small percentage of the proceeds of prize draws, raffles, bingo and anything that would bring in a little money.

The Club has managed to adapt with the years. Time changes most things: there are women members as well as the men, unheard of in the past, but very necessary for the future, all contributing where it matters most, coming in to have an occasional drink.

From its humble beginnings back in 1909, the Club has grown and given pleasure to many, providing leisure facilities and entertainment for men, women and children for most of this century. It would be a great loss should it cease to exist.

Let us hope that as we approach the millennium, the Club will see the next century out.

The Wheatsheaf 1999

The Wheatsheaf Public House

The Wheatsheaf 1916

Known as the Duke of Cleveland in 1832, this pub may well go back to 1750 or even further. It was a coaching stop and The Square, a group of buildings to the rear, may well have been stables in those days. The name changed to the Encombe Inn in 1902 and, by the First World War arrived, it bore its present name and is frequently referred to as "The Bush" by the locals.

The Wheatsheaf of today is a very different place both inside and out. It closed in 1995 for a major refurbishment, reopening on the 26th September 1995, boasting big-screen TV, darts, pool, function room, food lunch and evening, and live entertainment. A far cry from the spit-and-sawdust days our predecessors were used to, many years ago.

Chilton Miners' Welfare bowling green, tennis courts behind.

The Miners' Welfare 1924

The welfare was another step on the way to giving the miner and his family a much improved leisure environment. Miners' Colliery Welfares existed in other parts of the county and were sometimes referred to as the Colliery Welfare with CW often tagged on to the local village football team; for example, Murton CW.

As the mine production increased towards 1923/4, hope for a brighter future seemed possible. There was an application for permission to change an allotment garden into a tennis court and Pease and Partners, who now controlled Chilton, arranged to build a welfare ground for the workmen. The owners provided £3,500 towards it, the Miners' Welfare Fund £1,658, and the miners contributed a penny per ton of coal filled, from their wages. It opened in 1924, providing a football pitch in front of West Chilton Terrace, with a covered stand for the spectators and large changing rooms for the players. Close by, a cricket pitch, a bowling green, several tennis courts and a children's recreation ground were completed.

The Star Cinema occupied the first three houses in Durham Road. Built about 1915, they were showing coloured slides and silent movies. Mrs. Scrafton, who lived in Durham Road was the accompanying pianist, playing to suit the mood of the film. Not quite the marvel of modern-day cinema. However, it would be no less exciting for the audience of those far-off days.

Not all Beer and Skittles

In Chilton during the First World War a number of young men enlisted for the Armed Forces. In all there were 211: only half of these returned. The remainder were either killed in action or posted missing. Those who did return were offered their jobs back at the mine, at the usual rates. There were widows as a result of the war; they had no one to support them, but in this the owners of Chilton Pit were not lacking in charity. When the need arose, they allowed these women to live in their colliery houses rent-free. In some cases there were a number of children involved, the prospect being, as they became old enough, they would more than likely end up working at the pit.

Lady Sybil Eden received an OBE for running her hospital at Windlestone Hall. Many passed through her door to be cared for, who, in normal circumstances, would never have got anywhere near. Change was in the air; ordinary people, wounded or not, were now seeing the inside of these stately homes.

After the war, Chilton and Windlestone gradually returned to normal, but the upheaval and disturbance caused by it meant that things would never be quite the same again. The residents now had much more confidence in their ability to survive and were determined to decide their own destinies.

In 1918, the Durham Miners' Association looked upon Trade Unionism as the most important tool when it came to protecting the rights of the workers. The Union had steered clear of politics up until now. However, the ordinary man in the street wanted more representation. A new spirit had become apparent in the mining districts.

Ten miners' lodges ran their own candidates in the local elections on a Labour Party programme and returned a majority to power on the County Council. There was a redistribution of constituencies and Chilton lay in the Sedgefield District. For the first time, the local unions joined together to raise funds for their own candidate to contest the seat at the next General Election, and Chilton was no exception. The Sedgefield Divisional Labour Party was formed with direct support of the Durham Miners' Association. As a result of this, one of the first men to be selected as a candidate was a man living in Chilton, his name, John Herriotts.

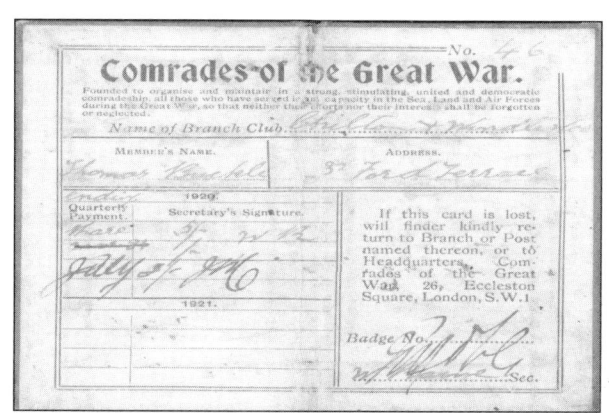

Chilton and Windlestone Comrades of the Great War Membership

B 132

WELCOME HOME.

Grand National,

Run ·March 28th, 1919.

First Prize, £4 0 0,   Third Prize, £1 0 0
Second ,,   2 10 0,   Fourth ,,   0 10 0

TICKETS 6D. EACH.

John Herriotts 1874 to 1935

John Herriotts taken from a Chilton Lodge Banner 1929 and may have coincided with his general election victory of the same year as the Labour Member of Parliament for the Sedgefield constituency.

*Checkweighman - Person appointed by the coal hewers (who paid his wages) to check the weight of full tubs as they came to the surface, to ensure correct weight and pay for coals filled.

The migration of the Herriotts family in search of work, to survive, was a common occurrence over the centuries. Their eventual arrival in Chilton only emphasises the lengths to which miners and their families would go to in order to survive, faced with the monumental decision to uproot and move on, in a harsh and unforgiving world.

John Herriotts was born in Tredegar, South Wales, on llth September 1874, the son of a miner. In the early part of the 1800s the family crossed the English Channel from Brittany to work in the tin mines of Cornwall. The family name at that time was thought to be Heriot. They then moved to South Wales to work in the coal mines there. In the Birth Register for that time, the father's name was given as Joseph Herriotes. Like the majority of miners' families in the later part of the 1870s, Johns family suffered serious poverty and hardship. Incidentally, his mother, as a young woman, had worked underground, drawing (pushing) tubs of coal.

With John only five years of age, his parents sold everything they had and bought a horse and cart to carry the children and what few belongings they could take with them, whilst they themselves walked all the way to the Durham Coalfield. They first settled in Ferryhill. John was educated at Board Schools, including Middlestone Moor, and became a pupil teacher at an early age. His strong-minded mother withdrew him from the school when his salary was stopped, brought about by the withdrawal of the schools grant by the Board. John then entered the mines but continued with his education, reading and attending WEA (educational) classes. He became a *Checkweighman, first at Binchester Colliery, which closed in 1908, then at Windlestone and Fishburn. He took an active part in Union business at branch level, whilst devoting time sitting on various wages boards. John was a member of the Executive Council of the Durham Miners' Association (DMA) and the Miners' Permanent Relief Fund.

After the First World War, he twice stood, unsuccessfully, for the position of Agent to the DMA in 1919 and 1926, being defeated on both occasions by James Gilliland.

From 1907 to 1910 he was a Durham County Councillor and became a Justice of the Peace in 1914, eventually becoming Chairman of the Bishop Auckland Magistrates, a position he held for many years. In the latter part of his life, until he died, he was a member of Sedgefield Rural District Council.

The wealth of experience gained from his involvement in a broad spectrum of local affairs was to become the springboard for the major political role of his life, and one that history would remember him by, that of the Labour Member of Parliament for Sedgefield.

Herriotts had joined the Independent Labour Party (ILP) as a young man and was energetic in the Bishop Auckland district attending as a delegate from Spennymoor to the ILPconference in l909. During the First World War he was Chairman of the Bishop Auckland Labour Party. His adoption as Labour candidate for the Sedgefield Constituency came towards the end of the war. John's fight to make and keep this constituency a Labour seat had remarkable ups and downs in the next twelve years.

The last banner made for Chilton Lodge.

The DMA, along with other areas in England, Scotland and Wales, joined together to form a formidable alliance, the National Union of Mineworkers. With the onset of the nationalisation of the mines they won many concessions and improvements for the miner, making his industry one of the safest in this modern day.

In the Coupon Election of 1918 Herriotts was beaten into second place by Col. Rowland Burdon (Con.Unionist).

The result was as follows:

Burdon Col. Rowland - Con Un 6,627

Herriotts John - Labour 5,801

Starmer Sir Charles - Liberal 3,333

Con. Un Maj. - 826

Herriotts was to have success in 1922 when he beat the Conservative candidate Eli Waddington and gained a majority of 729. Those results were as follows:

Herriotts J. - Lab. 9,796

Waddington E. - Con. 9,067

Brown C. H. - I. L. 3,561

Lab Maj. - 729

Success for John Herriotts was to be short-lived. In the following year, 1923, he was beaten in a straight fight with Major L. Ropner (Unionist), by six votes.

Ropner Maj. L. - Un. 11,093

Herriotts J. - Lab. 11,087

Unionist Maj 6

There were three recounts and several scrutinies, after 110 papers had been rejected as spoilt because they were not stamped. Herriotts lost by these six votes, and he was bitterly disappointed. He told a Durham Chronicle reporter: *"We are not satisfied with the decision. I am certain I would have won the seat, had not the unstamped papers been rejected."* At the election of 1924, as if to add salt to raw wounds Ropner increased his majority to 24. In 1929,with a national swing to Labour, Herriotts took the seat from Ropner, and he retained it for the following two years. All in all, John Herriotts, who lived in Eden Terrace, Chilton, had come a long way from the poverty he first grew up in, in South Wales, apparently a self-made man who worked tirelessly for the good of the people. Many of the unfortunates of that time would be pleased to have him on their side and he appears to have become the people's champion.

He is laid to rest in Chilton Cemetery, the first on the left, there is also a memorial plaque in St Aidan's Church, if one is interested.

His place on the Chilton Lodge Banner was well-earned and long may this banner be preserved where it is on public display in Chilton Junior School.

Chilton School Team 1931
back row l to r: *G. Foster, A. Philips, R. Smedley, W. G. Waite, (staff) R. Ashpool, H. Sullivan, T. Wilson* **sitting:** *W. Matthews, A. B. Ross (head), T. Langdale (capt), J. Nattrass (Staff), G. Gowland* **front:** *A. Wilson, M. Oliver*

Billy Matthews and his bride, late 1940s. Billy was a good bat, I remember him hitting one ball straight over West Chilton Terrace for six. He played football for Chilton Athletic at this time. He worked at Chilton Pit as a Deputy, living in Dene Bridge Row most of his life; he still lives in the village. Guard of honour, **left side first:** *Jack Cheesmond, Bob Morton, Tom Oyston.* **Right side:** *?, Alan Leighton, Sam Robinson. Page, Barry Matthews*

CHAPTER SIX

Rushyford

Rushyford

Approaching from the direction of Chilton, Rushyford still looks much as it always has dominated by an old Manor House (now the Eden Arms) adjoined by a row of houses dating back to the 18th century. It was once a busy coaching inn until the advent of the Darlington to Newcastle railway about 1840 and the emergence later on of motorised road transport.

The Edens had occupied their residence, the Manor House at West Auckland, since 1568. Over the years, as their Windlestone estates expanded, a permanent presence was required, with one of the houses there being adequate for their needs. In 1835, they refurbished the Elizabethan-style Manor House at Rushyford. It became home to the Edens on the estate at Windlestone for a few years while their house was pulled down to make way for the almost palatial new house, Windlestone Hall, completed in 1855. The 6th Baronet, Sir William Eden, moved from West Auckland and took up residence at Windlestone when the Hall was completed.

Lady Francis Sybil Eden lived in the Manor House at Rushyford after the death of her husband, Sir William, the 7th Baronet, in 1915. The Eden Arms of the 1800s, was situated at the north end of the adjoining row and, for a short time was known as the Wheatsheaf. The yard to the rear had coach houses and stables, some dating from the mid-1700s.

You may recall the first Lord Eldon, John Scott (1751 - 1838). He stayed over on many occasions at the old Eden Arms, and it became one of his favourite places, probably having a lot to do with good food and, more importantly, what was in the cellar.

The Manor House and adjoining buildings

The cottages by the side of the old road to Bishop Auckland, with Rushyford School in the background, to the right. Mr. Joseph Welch, a former headmaster of the school, lived in one of them.

An Ambush at Rushyford in the 13th Century

On the eve of a winter's day when George III was King, a horseman travelling on the Great North Road saw in the gathering gloom, signs of a coming storm. When darkness fell, the wind rose, bringing showers of stinging sleet.He passed Ferryhill, with the gale increasing to a blizzard, the sleet turning into snow, swirling around his horse and already forming drifts upon the frozen road.

Rushyford, 1890s, traps and carts awaiting repairs outside the blacksmith's shop

Presently, the man was glad to hear the blast of a bugle above the noise of the storm, arriving in time to see travellers alighting from a stagecoach standing at the door of a huge inn in the valley of Rushyford. The man greeted his fellow travellers and expressed his intention of venturing no further that night. They replied with one accord that such was their decision.

After seeing to the needs of his horse, and his stomach warmed with a glass of mulled ale, he later on joined the company sitting by the fire in the bar parlour. Most of them were sitting smoking churchwarden pipes and drinking hot rum or whiskey toddies, the topic of conversation being the perils of the road. After listening to some hair-raising accounts of footpads and highwaymen, the man interested the company with the following account.

How, at Rushyford in 1318, Louis de Beaumont was on his way to take up his new appointment as Lord Bishop of Durham. Louis was said to be a foreigner and his selection was not popular in the North, where the Prince Bishop ruled this area with all the power of a monarch. The King's opponents decided to delay the Bishop until after the harvest, a great deal of the money raised from the harvest would be taken by the Bishop in tithes and taxes, which, the people felt was rightfully theirs.

The ambush was planned to be at Rushyford. The Bishop, accompanied by his brother and two cardinals, were seized by what appeared to be a band of marauders under the command of Gilbert Middleton of Northumberland. Middleton was dismayed, to say the least, on seeing the cardinals. He immediately set them free, as it was forbidden to harm them, they being appointees of the Pope. Never-the-less,he carried off the Bishop and his brother and imprisoned them in Mitford Castle, Northumberland, Middleton's home, demanding a heavy ransom for their release. The cardinals, on their arrival at Durham Cathedral, took the Cathedral's treasure and exchanged it for the safe release of Louis. He was eventually consecrated Bishop of Durham in 1318, a position he held until his death 15 years later.

What of Middleton? His castle was surrounded by followers of the King. When captured, he was executed and his body cut up and sent to different parts of the country as a warning to those who would oppose the wishes of the King.

The main entrance to Rushyford from the Great North Road, now the A167, was over the bridge spanning the Black Beck. Partially hidden by trees is the original Eden Arms. Around 1890, Arthur Thompson and Harry Johnson, estate workers, are taking time off on the bridge.

The row of cottages in the background is now over 200 years old and housed employees and their families working on the Windlestone Estate. One cottage, to the far left, doubled as a post office run by Isabella Hunter in 1900, with a small counter just inside the front door and taking up part of the front room. The tradition was carried on by her daughter, Jane Aldred, in 1950 for another 39 years. It closed in 1989 with the distinction of being the smallest post office in England.

A blacksmith's shop stood at the opposite end, near to the Black Beck. It served the needs of stage coaches, repairing their wooden spoke wheels and fitting new steel tyres, sometimes a complete new wheel. There would be frequent casualties from the ruts and potholes of those old, unmade roads. A ready trade in horse shoeing would ensure it being a thriving business.

A two-wheeled cart, with wooden wheels shown to good effect. A common sight on farms for hundreds of years, used for everything from manure to vegetables.

Arthur Thompson and Harry Johnson, estate workers, take time off on the bridge

The Landlord of the Eden Arms in the 1890's was Edward Johnson, shows a dray wagon on the left. The lady and children may well include some of his family.

A number of wheels were still being made and repaired for farmers, milkmen greengrocers and the like, who still used carts and traps during the Second World War 1939-45. It closed about 1950. The horse and cart were typical of many seen around the farms and villages in those times. Bob Johnson is the man holding the reins; he and his brother, Edward (publican), ran a farm on the Eden Estate. The four-wheeled flat carts shown were ideal, well-suited to the breweries as dray wagons. Household removals and almost anything would be moved on one of those carts before the combustion engine appeared on the scene.

Until the beginning of coal mining in the locality, Rushyford may well have had both post office and school, before the like appeared in Chilton Buildings. The school was situated to the rear of the blacksmith's shop, close to the beck. Both are long gone, in their place is a modern children's nursery. The new school, built in stone and sited at the top of a small rise to the rear of the Eden Arms, was in use at the turn of the century and closed about 1946.

Rushyford School 1901. The little girl looking away on the left of the picture is Margaret Johnson, daughter of Edward Johnson, landlord of the Eden Arms. It is Margaret's daughter, Mrs. Margaret Robinson of Kirk Merrington, whose photographs are reproduced here.

The headmaster for many years was Joseph Welch, who lived in one of the cottages further on past the school. Mr. Welch was an ever-present member of the congregation at Windlestone Wesleyan Methodist Chapel to the rear of New South View, where he preached as well as taking children's Sunday School.

The pace of change in the early part of the century was slow, as it always had been, but times were to change dramatically in the 1930s. The fortunes of the all-powerful Edens were being reduced on three fronts.

Surtax rates increased in 1929 and death duties were taking their toll as well. By 1931, the loss of tonnage rent and certain rent (annual) from the lease on the closure of Windlestone Colliery brought forward the day when some of the surplus furniture and china were sold, probably to make ends meet.

Finally, in 1936, Sir Timothy the 8th Baronet put the entire estate up for sale. It took place at the Kings Head Hotel, Darlington.

A Summary of the Estate

4,000 acres, 20 Mixed Farms, Numerous Smallholdings, Attractive Residences, Building and Accommodation Land, 2 licensed Public houses, The Eden Arms (Rushyford), The Eden Arms (Leasingthorne). Shops, Allotment Gardens, Cottages and Ground Rents. There were many more items, too numerous to mention. In the

The estate workers cottages which became lots 43, 44, 45A in the great sale.

great sale, the estate workers' cottages became Lots 43, 44, 45 and 45A. Lot 45 was the post office, described as an adjoining cottage with excellent gardens, covering an area of 24 poles, in the Parish of Windlestone. Occupied by Mrs. Aldred.

The North Eastern Brewery Company were successful with their bid in the 1936 sale for the Eden Arms and adjoining row, lot 39; it cost them £6,500. It is possible the name changed at this time to the Wheatsheaf for a few years, reverting to its original name when the Manor House and the Public House were combined to form the splendid hotel that we see today.

The Eden Arms 1910, with the old and new transport parked outside

Windlestone Cottage, part of the Eden Estate and occupied by one of the gamekeepers. Situated on the right side of the road 100 yards past Windlestone Hall gates, it was demolished to make way for a new road about 1980.

Rushyford School House, formerly the school, now an attractive private residence

Rushyford School became Lot 48, with adjoining playing field area, covering 3 roods 16 poles, in the Parish of Windlestone. Let to the Durham County Council on a lease at £13 6s.0d per annum (including water), terminating 30th of July 1953, determinable by Lessees giving 6 months' notice from any time. See Lot 49 as to Right of Way.

The Elizabethan lines of the Eden Arms Hotel, Rushyford, shown to good effect on a summer's morning in 1999. Little changed outwardly, the interior is a large, deluxe hotel owned by the Swallow group, catering for the most discerning traveller.

CHAPTER SEVEN

A Time of Depression

A Time of Depression

The 1920s

The mine owners and the men relied on a steady market for the coal they produced at Chilton and Windlestone. If the mine made a profit, the men got their pay. The union was there to ensure the pitmen got a fair crack of the whip and were not taken advantage of. In the 1920s the industrial climate began to change, with economic difficulties facing the whole country, and with coal mining not the least affected. Even more so, for our relatively young village, culminating in a drop in population. Many people suffered constant hardship, sometimes for years.

In 1921, the mines production dropped. There was a General Strike for eighty days, referred to as the 21st strike, causing friction in the village. During this time, only one-seventh of the coal drawn from the two pits was taken

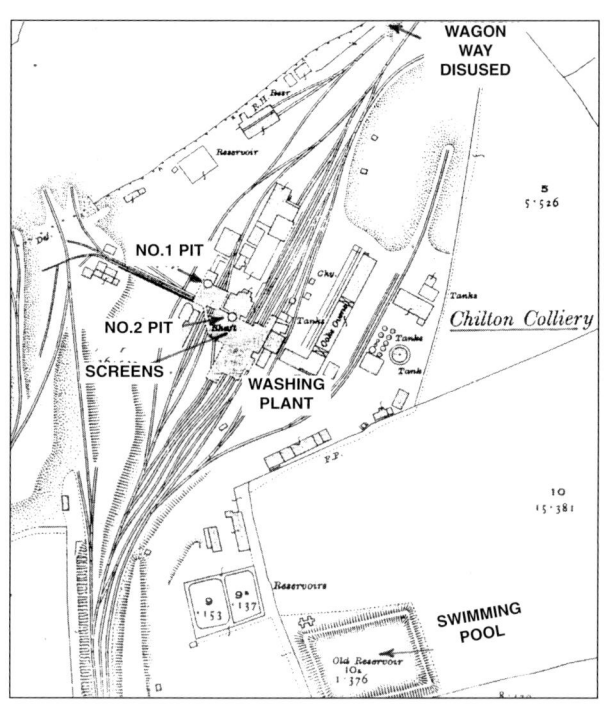

Chilton Colliery 1920

away and sold, miners were being laid off and feelings were intense. The following year, coal production increased. There were no strikes, but the number in employment dropped, with the situation still looking black for the miners.

By 1923, this had changed. Production and employment increased rapidly, brought about by a general improvement nationally. Most of us are aware of the saying "success is sometimes brought about by the downfall of others". The improved state of the coal industry was caused by a sixteen-week coal strike in America in 1922, and the French occupation of the Ruhr coalmining area of Germany, which was responsible for an increase in the demand for British coal.

However, by the end of the year, the third shift of the day at Chilton Pit was stopped and production decreased once more. The situation was not to improve for some years.

*Oil lamps are safety
lamps,commonly referred
to as "Oilies".*

*This group of miners are sitting in Chilton Colly pit yard, waiting to start their shift about 1921/22. They
used oil lamps* in those days, to see and to work. The miners here are:* **l to r:** *Lou Boycott (Windlestone),
Ernie Hope (Chilton), Mr.Mc.Manners (Coundon), Alec Mathews and Tom Stanwick, both from Chilton.*

The 1920s

The very name, safety lamp, says it all. A lamp which is safe for the miner to use underground
which will not ignite firedamp (methane), a gas which seeps out of the coal.

Until the oil lamps were introduced to replace the naked flame of the candle, the amount of
deaths underground in coal mines due to explosions ran into many thousands and were
commonplace.

Happy Days

The Cork Club: an odd name, but then, there was a "Dicky Bow Club" where the members
had to wear a bow tie at their gatherings. They were all members of Chilton Club. The Cork
Club may well have been in similar vein and probably drew its members from the local
workingmen's clubs. Benny Mathews, a retired ex-Windlestone and Fishburn miner, formerly
of South View, explained that these men taken at Ferryhill Station, were miners from Chilton
and Mainsforth Collieries. His brother, Alec Mathews is the man in the middle, squatting. He
is also seen above in Chilton pit yard.

The assortment of head gear worn is particularly interesting, flat caps, bowler hats (similar to
Charlie Chaplin's), trilby hats and straw hats (boaters) reminding one of cruising down the
river on a Sunday afternoon.

*The Cork Club outing around
1922*

Even so, they look a tidy bunch. They will have raised the money for the trip from raffles and prize draws and would, no doubt, enjoy themselves, the pit being the last thing in their minds. The vehicle looks magnificent, with its solid wheels and brass, carbide gas headlights. Should it rain, there are plenty helpers to pull forward the massive hood at the rear of the bus.

Pease and Partners take over Chilton Colliery

Not so much a takeover, in the modern-day sense, but the outcome was to be much the same. In 1924, the year of Chilton RA's. record season, change was in the air at the mine. Henry Stobart and Co, the owners for 24 years and a major benefactor to the village, became a subsidiary of Pease and Partners, with the name of Stobart retained.

Pease now had the missing link in the major exploitation of the deeper seams in the area, namely the Harvey, Busty and Brockwell. With Chilton now joining Eldon and Windlestone pits under the same ownership, it would not be too long before the barrier coal separating Chilton and Windlestone pits would be taken out.

Eldon Colliery had, by this time, progressed east in the Brockwell seam. Their underground roadways eventually joined with Windlestone, who were working in a westerly direction, towards them. Windlestone Pit was still winding coal to the surface, but not for much longer. As soon as the roadways through the barrier coal between the two pits were completed, coal winding would cease at the Windlestone end of what would become a combined mine.

Windlestone Colliery about 1916. The houses seen in the background are in Durham Road.

When the new roadways were completed through to the Windlestone workings from Chilton, coal would be hauled to Chilton shaft Harvey level, to be drawn to the surface. The facilities for screening,washing and coking Windlestone coal were capable of handling the production from both collieries. There was, however, another important reason why all this should be happening and why Chilton Pit should survive at the expense of Windlestone.

Chilton had two extra-thick seams of workable coal which were not in evidence in the Windlestone shaft, namely the Five Quarter and Main Coal, both of which were 1.5 metres in thickness approximately. Therefore, Chilton appeared to be the most viable option in view of its larger coal reserves, which, in turn, should give the miners working there and at Windlestone a more secure future.

For the time being though, it was business as usual at Windlestone, who were now working the Harvey seam as well as the Brockwell. The Harvey seam is 266 feet (81m) above the Brockwell. To gain access to the Harvey, an inclined roadway (tunnel) had to be blasted through the rock approximately 435 yards (402m) long, from the Brockwell level. As the Harvey developed, the tubs filled in this seam were lowered down the

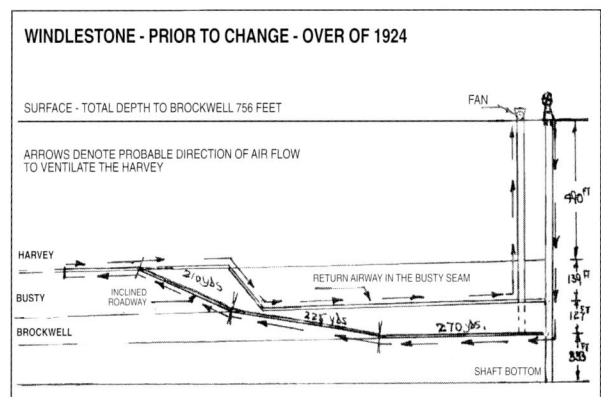

Windlestone's Harvey Drift (inclined roadway)

inclined roadway to the Brockwell level, at a point approximately 270 yards (249m) away from the shaft. From there, they would be hauled along to the shaft and drawn to the surface.

Mining operations are carefully planned years in advance before being put into practice. Underground surveyors with their sometimes bulky, but precise equipment, plan the direction and inclination, that roadways must take, so that when they are completed they are in exactly the right place.

There were disputes and grievances at the pit between the men and the owners. The union would put the case to the Durham Coal Owners Association; sometimes they won, and at other times they would lose.

One such case may be of interest to the reader. "The colliery manager at Windlestone sent home the following stonemen and *shifters, without pay, who presented themselves at work on Good Friday, April 14th 1911, at 10.30pm, in accordance with the custom of the colliery.

Shifter: Well named, this man's job was to shift anything required to be moved, underground, to a new location and make ready for the next shift, following on.

The Union asked that he be ordered to pay each man his shift. The men involved were: Stonemen: W. Jackson, W. Henderson and J. Adams. Shifters: H. Easter, J. Holmes, J. Stephenson, F. Prior, G. Goundry, J. Raine, W. Evans, L. Hall and E. Ayre. The result - Settled - Each man was paid his shift."

Roadways, Tubs and Haulage

By far the best way to visualise a roadway, tubs or haulage as part of the miners' daily routine, is with a photograph or a drawing. The following should do much to enlighten those who have never seen a coal mine.

This roadway is supported by arched girders. The conveyor on the right is transporting the coal from the mine workings further in (inbye), to a point where it will be loaded into tubs on its way out (outbye) to the surface. The track on the left is for transporting equipment in tubs, such as wooden props and planks etc.

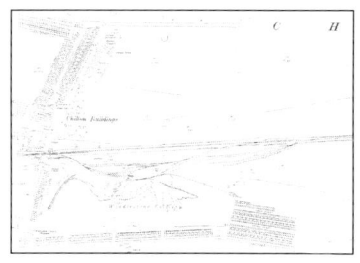

Windlestone Colliery in 1919, when the pit was at its peak. An increase in the number of railway sidings to cope with larger tonnages of coal ,and an increase in miners' houses, was a sign of those times.
(enlarged for more detail on page 138)

This set has just emerged from a tunnel (roadway) in the hillside to the rear. Not all mines have pit shafts, this is a drift mine.

Tubs

Where there are no conveyors, tubs are used at all times. The curving roadway is supported by straight girders and shows tubs with corrugated sheets and trams (a longer version of the tub), loaded with girders, going inbye to support the roof. A number of tubs is called a set: there could be as few as 10 or as many as 60, all coupled together.

Haulage

The engine required to do this kind of work is bolted down onto a

heavy-duty steel girder frame, which, in turn, is bolted to a thick concrete foundation.The photograph below shows the upper half of a haulage engine in use, powered in this case by a l00 hp·electric motor. The motor's power is transmitted through a set of reduction gears designed to allow the engine to perform its task. These 6 feet diameter steel rope drums, seen here, can revolve to give a speed of up to 8 mph, it being the maximum allowed for this engine hauling tubs. In this instance, the distance hauled is 1.25 miles, from underground to the surface. The white steel uprights, in the foreground, with long tie rods attached to them, are brake shoes. They are linked to a foot pedal close to the person operating the engine. He is the "hauler braker" and very aptly named.

Chilton and Windlestone pits had similar haulage engines up to 300 hp. When one considers the load being pulled, as many as 60 tubs, each one with half a ton of coal in it, and added to this, the distance hauled, probably upwards of two miles. Both pits were working quite near to Windlestone Hall, in different seams; this gives an indication of the work done by these massive engines.

The author operating this engine in 1993

At Chilton and Windlestone, with the coal seams being a good depth from the surface, shafts were sunk to reach them. In the photograph, right, the coal seam is nearer to the surface and only required these two tunnels (roadways) be made into the hillside to reach the coal.

For the residents of the village, conditions continued to fluctuate during the 1920s with everything hinging on the mines' performance. This decade produced a mixture of hope and despair, brought about mainly by depressions within the mining industry. Finding alternative employment was difficult, almost impossible, for the miner who found himself laid off. However, some work did come the miners' way, as the Council Minutes Book for October 1921 shows. **"The clerk was instructed to draw Mr. Lodge's attention to the urgent need of finding employment for a good number of men that were out of work. He pointed out that there were several roads which were scheduled to be made."**

Money was made available and groups of men, mainly miners, were given employment upgrading roads and constructing new ones.

School attendances dropped from 829 in 1922 to 723 in 1926, reflecting the difficulties of the time, with some people migrating south to seek work.

The village, however, continued to grow, if not in size, in importance. In 1920, new train services began from Ferryhill Station at the request of the local council. Chilton soon had easy access to Darlington, York, Newcastle, Stockton and North Shields, while local services were extended. Bus services were developed and provided a vital local service. They ran to many of the surrounding villages about once every hour.

This group of men were a common sight in the 1920s, posing beside their cement mixer and aggregates

It appears to be a wet and miserable day and not very grand, as one can see. But then, mining was never picturesque.

An early bus timetable

Meanwhile, underground at Chilton, they were driving new roadways through the barrier coal separating Chilton from Windlestone. This would happen in a relatively short time, a matter of weeks. Windlestone coal would then be rerouted, as it were, along the new roadways, to the Harvey level of No.1 Shaft at Chilton and then drawn to the surface.

This view of the latticed winding headgear at No.1 Pit, Chilton

With the coupling together of Chilton and Windlestone, it was now possible to walk underground between the two pits, through the new roadways. From there it was also possible to carry on walking in a westerly direction through the main roadways of Windlestone and Eldon, where one would eventually arrive at Eldon shaft. This was possible, so long as the pumps at Eldon shaft bottom continued to operate, keeping the water below the Brockwell seam level to avoid flooding.

Problems Underground

Ventilating the many underground roadways from Eldon to Windlestone had become increasingly difficult. To alleviate this situation, it was decided that a new concrete pit headgear be built at the top of the main shaft, replacing the wooden structure that had been in use since the sinking of the pit in 1872. A large ventilating fan was then installed to improve the flow of air around the mines.

As part of the overall strategy, the winding of coal to the surface at Windlestone would cease, to make way for the fan, and, in doing so, would bring about the closure of Windlestone Pit.

The writing had been on the wall for some years; even so, it would still be quite a blow, especially to those men who worked on the surface. They lost their jobs. Most of the mine buildings remained, but there was little or no activity. The community probably accepted the situation more readily, knowing that the men with jobs underground would be kept on, their work still available in the Brockwell and Harvey seams.

Prospect Terrace, Arthur and Albert Streets

Windlestone Colliery Epitaph

All things have their day; people come and go, some leaving a lasting memory, an example for those who follow them. Pits are no different. They contributed and were the hub of a community, the like of which, is fast fading, in this modern day and age and will not be seen again. The space, or if you like, the slot in time, for Windlestone Colliery was from 1877 when the shafts were completed, to 1924 when coal winding ceased. The miners who worked there have passed on, along with the first houses built for the pit, being Windlestone Row, later to become South View. However, there are still monuments to the pit remaining: New South View; the Miners' Institute, now the Catholic Church; and the Memorial Cottages just below, in Brooklyn Road. Prospect Terrace, and Arthur and Albert Streets also stand as testimony to that period of time.

So it was with Windlestone Pit. It provided the work that gave birth to a village, and the houses which surrounded the pit on three sides, with the railway to the north, were home to hundreds of miners, their wives and children.

They lived and played around the perimeter of the stone heaps, a proud bunch of people who survived in a much harsher environment than the one we know today, and from whom a good number of the community are descended.

Windlestone Colliery showing the new totally-enclosed concrete headgear and adjoining fan house shortly after being installed 1924/5. The steam winder was used only for men descending to their work.

Many will take pride in what they achieved, those people who, in the beginning, first breathed life into Windlestone Village and set it on the road to posterity. Men, women and children, able to keep their heads up even when times could get no worse; they carried on and eventually won the fight to give us part of our heritage.

The National Strike 1926

The illusive "feel good factor", pursued by many in these modern times, is sometimes fleeting and gone before we even realise it. So, it would seem, was the situation from 1924 to 1926. With the Miners' Welfare opened only a short while and our football team doing so well, it was a bitter blow to find that 500 miners were being finished at Chilton.

Windlestone Colliery, at its peak about 1915/18, owned by Joseph Pease and Partners of Darlington. Taken from a position approximately 80 metres to the rear of Chilton Branch Library.

Coal production in 1925 reached its lowest level since the mine was opened in 1902. Living conditions in the village were not good, but there were no strikes. Those still working were afraid of losing their jobs if they made any protests. The situation at Chilton was echoed all over the country, with another depression biting hard. Peases had managed to keep Chilton

A sign of the times, the "soup kitchens", a common sight during the 1926 National Strike and for a while after. This classroom at Chilton school is also typical, soup being served by the staff, assisted by striking miners and their wives.

pit open albeit on reduced manpower. However, the 1926 national strike was just around the corner and this brought the pit to a standstill.

For years it had been a struggle; now the picture was very bleak indeed. With only the meagre Relief Allowance to live on, miners could not even afford the rent on their allotment gardens. The Council were well aware of the men's plight and of the consequences should anyone be turned off their allotment, knowing full-well that the produce grown went a long way to supplement the family diet. To avoid a near desperate situation getting any worse, the Council took the sympathetic view and turned no one off his allotment, with the rent arrears cancelled. Some of these men had been out of work for six months, while a number finished at Windlestone had not worked for two years. As unemployment grew and money became scarce, particularly during the strike, many things changed.

The railway crossing

Where it was always the wealthier people in the village who played tennis, with the correct kit worn at all times, the Recreation's facilities were open to everyone; even those children wearing boots were allowed to play tennis.

Men stood around corner ends with nothing to do. A few would end up in the Recreation Club, playing billiards to pass the time away, sometimes for only a penny a game, but the rivalry was intense. It was not uncommon for some to fall out with each other after losing the game.

The railway crossing was out of use during the strike. It carried coals from Coundon and Westerton area in the mid 1800s. It was used extensively by Leasingthorne until 1949/50, and by Chilton for the last time on Friday, December 2nd 1960. From this time, coals were transported underground through a system of conveyor and locomotive roadways to Dean and Chapter colliery at Ferryhill, via Leasingthorne. As one might imagine, it was quite an undertaking, if I may use the phrase.

The Local Authority realised the problems that would arise from enforced idleness and no money, and set about organising a series of events to help pass the time. Competitions were organised for small prizes, to provide entertainment for the unemployed. Football contests, walking and running races, tug of war and bowling or throwing a cricket ball, were all played for food vouchers. All of these activities, to try and keep everyone's spirits up. Hiking and walking provided a welcome change and helped one to forget their predicament, at least for a while.

Poaching was rampant, brought about by the sheer necessity to keep one's family fed. The Eden estate was no longer out of bounds; Sir Timothy Eden was well aware of the miners' plight. His position now weakened financially by death duties and taxes, he was not able, nor had he any intentions of stopping the intrusions onto his land.

As for fuel to keep the home fires burning, children made their contribution by collecting wood from anywhere they could find it, including the Windlestone Estate. Inevitably, a small amount of coal got mixed in with the stone,during mining operations and could not be separated. This was tipped, with the stone which formed the sometimes gigantic stone heap, next to the mine. It was here the boys and girls could be found, sorting the coal from the stone, to take home for the fire.

All in all, what with poaching, stealing vegetables and fruit from the local farmers, plus that which came from the allotments, families just managed to keep from starving. Hard times indeed.

After the Strike

A sigh of relief would be felt by all when the strike ended. The mine reopened and production began to rise; this trend continued for the next few years. Men lined up for work but not all of them were set back on, with hundreds still on Parish Relief, so it was far from being the perfect solution.

Miners cycled or walked to neighbouring collieries, such as Dean and Chapter, Mainsforth, Thrislington (the site is now Banks Bros. Haulage and Mining, at

The Great North Road through Chilton. Horse and traps and a bicycle are a far cry from our clogged roads of today. The wood and tin church of St.Aidan, burnt down in 1928 Chilton Council School on the left and Eden Terrace 1915 on the right, gave us a time around the 1920s.

West Cornforth), and Fishburn to see if there was any work. The lucky ones who got a job had to cycle or walk to work from Chilton, rain, hail or shine. One such person was Jimmy Carney. He had a struggle to get to work, way back in the 1920/30s; not very tall, about 5ft 2ins in height, stocky in build, with a broad face and white hair combed straight back. His eyes, deep set, still had a sparkle when remembering the old days, the days when you never gave up, no matter what.

I met with him, quite by chance, walking with the help of a stick along the Main Street in Chilton. He was going for his pension. It was 2nd November 1995 and he was 87 years old. I asked how he was keeping. He said he was'nt so bad, but wished his wife was a little better, as she had been poorly for some time.

He started his working life at Adelaide Colliery, situated halfway up Busty Bank between South Church and Shildon, when he was fourteen, in 1923. The pit closed in 1924, from which he managed to get set on at Eldon Colliery, near Close House. He was walking to work in those days, until he got a bike, I think he said, from Bishop Auckland.

"Were you there long?" I asked him. "No, the pit closed in 1930 and I was lucky to get a job at Doggy (Thrislington). At that time I was married and biking from West Auckland to Doggy nearly every day of the week and working shifts. I eventually got a job at Chilton Pit and a house at Chilton, so I was set for life."

I remembered him working in the Main Coal Seam when I was at Chilton Pit in 1956. Jim continued, "I was a *Deputy and *Shotfirer then, the best job I ever had."

I made the comment that pit work must have agreed with him. "Well, I have worked hard all my life and I am still here - 87 year old, and very likely the only man alive now who worked at Adelaide Pit. All you need is a bit of luck, Brian, and you'll get by. I'll have to go, son, it's getting a bit chilly and I'd better get back to see how the wife is. See you." "Aye, Jim, see you later," I replied.

Every Picture Tells A Story

One of the earlier photographs, Chilton Lodge Banner at the Durham Miners' Gala about 1925, created a lot of interest. While identifying faces, a few of those revealed were youthful images of men I had known some 30 years later and approaching the end of their working days, in their late 50/60s in my time underground at Chilton Pit in the 1950's and 60s. It is amazing: identification was made in 1997, bridging a gap of more than 70 years. They have all passed on and are virtually forgotten now; all the more so I will endeavour to describe one or two of those I remember. But first, the photo and the roll call.

LOT 55
(Coloured Mauve on Plan No. 1).

The Site of Windlestone Colliery

extending in all to about
27a.   1r.   15p.

and upon which stand numerous Buildings.

Being part Ord. No. 181 and 176a in Chilton Parish and let to various tenants at rents totalling to £12 5s. 0d. per annum, and the North-Eastern Electric Supply Co. pay a way-leave of £17 10s. 0d. per annum for a power-house and Kiosk on this Lot.

Apportioned Outgoings:—
   Tithe (commuted): £4 0s. 8d.
   Land Tax, as assessed, if any.
   Rent Charge: £22.

See Stipulation No. 6 as to Electric Overhead Cables.

The auction of Windlestone Colliery

Standing: 2nd left, Fred Allison (Codger) who is remembered on page 125 Standing: 1st from the rt: *Jimmy Hamilton (Dene Bridge)* **5th rt:** *Joe Dinsley (Master Shifter)* **6th rt:** *Garnett Harker (Dene Terr.),* **7th rt: Jimmy Hall also remembered on page 125, 8th rt:** *Steve Hall,* **11th rt:** *Mr. Walker, all West Chilton Terr.* **Sitting:-1st left:** *Fred Taylor,* **2nd left:** *Jack Donald (West Chilton),* **4th left**: *Andrew Kennedy, then bandsmen, then John Tate and Jack Hillary, treasurer and secretary of Chilton Lodge.*

*A Deputy is responsible for the health and safety of the men in his charge, in an area underground usually called a district. As the name implies, he was deputised to act on behalf of the mine manager.

*A Shotfirer was similarly qualified, although his first obligation was the firing (blasting) of coal or stone, in the district he was assigned to.

*Caught by surprise, Codger, with a straight face, in his element with a tray of pints in Chilton Club, probably back from a funeral with his black silk scarf. **l to r:** Mock Burnett, Billy Neal **standing:** Jimmy Thompson (Slaughter's son)*

John Payton, stockily built and now in his 70s is a long-time resident of both Chilton and Windlestone. He served in the Army (DLI) during the World War II, returning to pitwork after it was over, working on the coal cutting machines. He took a long look at the Gala Day picture, commenting that the band was most probably regimental and hired in specially for the occasion. John noticed the stripes worn and the medals displayed on their tunics and the cap badge. He was of the opinion that it was not unlike the Royal Artillery. There are two persons from this picture, those in bold print, who, I have good reason to remember.

Fred Allison (Codger)

Fred was well known in the village, a real character. Not very tall and of average build for his height, he struck me as a happy, friendly person. He dressed in the manner of many of his generation white shirt (minus the loose collar) fastened at the neck with a collar stud, a navy-blue suit and waistcoat to match. A white silk scarf (normal), black scarf for funerals, knotted at the neck and, of course, the immortal flat cap and black leather boots, completed what was for many, a pitman's dress uniform.

He loved the countryside, was an expert on pheasants and rabbits, and known to be a good poacher, he was never caught. Remembering the hard times, there would not be many who hadn't tried their hand at a bit of poaching at one time or another. The mushroom fields were also Codger's domain and, though game was a necessity for the dinner table, it is not surprising to find he had a love of animals in his job as a horsekeeper in the stables underground at Chilton Pit.

There were more than sixty ponies underground at Chilton, even in my time, well looked after, hosed down, groomed and well fed after each shift. For all that, it was no bed of roses for the ponies, who were worked hard by men whose wages depended on how many tubs of coal they could bring out of the workings. Most miners looked after their ponies, but there was always a minority who would have them pull more than they were able, with some ponies taking a beating. In most of these cases, the man probably got away with it, the pony had an accident. Ponies were often referred to as Galloways (Gallawaz); presumably, at one stage, the stock would come from the Galloway region of Southern Scotland. A blacksmith came at regular intervals to renew worn shoes and, as the ponies coats became shaggy causing them to sweat more, the horsekeepers would *set to with the shears. After their trim they used to look very smart.

A Cut Below

One amusing memory that will always stay with me has Codger in what can only be described as a starring role. I was pony putting, in the Main Coal seam, bringing full tubs out and taking the empties back inbye for the coal hewers. My pony's name was Glen. He collided with a roof support girder with his forehead, resulting in a nasty gash that needed to be stitched. I walked him back to the stables over a mile away. It was the middle of the shift

When I arrived there, all was quiet. On walking along the rows of stalls, some occupied by resting ponies, I could hear a small whirring sound and came upon a stall occupied by three horsekeepers. The first of these turned the handle of a flexible drive with the pony shears fixed to the end. It was mounted on a tripod and held to the ground by standing on

Codger, supping his pint, with a smile back on his face

two of its legs with both feet, to keep it steady. The second keeper, his name was Edgar, was doing an excellent job of shearing. The third keeper, Codger Allison, sat on a three-legged stool, his pit helmet to one side. He was not quite bald and had a little hair around his ears and neck. Edgar was doing a near-perfect job of trimming with shears three times the size a hairdresser would use, while Codger sat, unconcerned, enjoying a free haircut. What a picture! What a photograph that would have been!

Jimmy Hall

Jimmy worked at Chilton most of his life, first as a *pieceworker, then a Deputy, and later on became a *Master Shifter, eventually returning to piecework, a job he liked and did well. He chose eight experienced, reliable men to work with him three on each shift to cover a full working day; they were known as Hall's Set.

There were a number of similar sets working underground at Chilton. Taylor's and Ward's were two of them, employed to make new roadways in any part of the mine where the need arose. Hall's had an excellent record for a job well done. When the momentous decision was taken in 1958/9 to drive new roadways underground to transport Chilton's coal production to Dene and Chapter Pit at Ferryhill using conveyor belt and locomotive haulage, Hall's were involved from the very beginning.

An Historic Moment

At this time I was very fortunate to have been selected to work with, and to learn the skills of, a miner from Hall's Set. After many months of tunnelling, the day finally came when the last roadway to be completed was only three metres away from another roadway coming towards us. Work was suspended at the other side to allow us to blast a way through the rock and make a connection. The time was 6 am. We drilled holes into the rock, filled each hole with explosives and an electric detonator, then retreated to a safe place. The shotfirer coupled the wires of each detonator together and, in turn, to a long cable, enabling him to retreat to a safe place. Now the other end of the cable was connected to a special battery designed to activate the explosives. One press of a button and BANG!

Set to: Get on with the job.

Master shifter: A Deputy, in charge of all the shifters.

Piecework: After completing a minimum task, eg coal filled or rock removed, all extra work attracted an agreed bonus.

Tons of rock were loose in seconds. We repeated this operation three times. After clearing the rock away for the third time, we found we had actually blasted a small hole through to the other side. We could see a number of lights moving about, worn by men from Leasingthorne Colliery, also part of Dene and Chapter.

We made the hole safe for a person to crawl through, taking down any loose or overhanging rock Jimmy Hall was on another shift and missed the sense of occasion we experienced. My workmates, Alec Hosie from Chilton and Ted Woodward from Auckland Park, shared this historic moment with me, as the first man to enter Chilton Pit from Leasingthorne crawled into our side of the tunnel, said "good morning" and shook our hands.

It wasn't just anyone. Con Mattimoe, at 61, was one of the old-style senior overman in charge of underground operations at Leasingthorne. His dress summed up his importance, wearing a short coat with a leather back to turn any roof water, knee breeches fastened below the knee, and long pit stockings, all navy blue. His white scarf, knotted at the neck, and steel toe capped boots completed, the attire of this man. The electric lamp he carried was also a spotlight, enabling him to see a hundred metres wherever he directed the beam. His safety oil lamp was polished and gleamed in the reflection of our own cap lamps.

Finally, he carried his pit stick, one yard in length, used to measure the advance of roadways, and for poking about to ensure work had been done to his satisfaction. Con Mattimoe was the kind of man used to giving orders and having them carried out without question. I knew him quite well; he lived in Windsor Terrace, Leeholme.

Mining is not without accidents, sometimes fatal. Jimmy Hall was a member of the Rescue Brigade. He, along with other dedicated miners, were willing to train for those sombre occasions when an explosion or a rock fall had occurred and help was needed desperately and quickly, to save the lives of men trapped and injured underground..

In this picture Jimmy is standing, third from the left at Crook Mines Rescue Station in the early 1930s. They are all wearing breathing apparatus, for use underground where there may be poisonous gases, especially after an explosion. The canaries in the cage on the wall would go with them, being the first to be affected, should the air be harmful, giving a warning to the rescuers and so help to save lives.

*Crook Miners' Rescue Station in the 1930s, situated at the bottom of Billy Row Bank. Shows instructors and trainees, with **Jimmy Hall standing 3rd from the left.***

The Unwanted Legacy

During the Great Strike of 1926, the underground workings at Eldon Colliery were "standing badly" due to the prolonged stoppage. In simple terms, the roof was collapsing in some areas of the mine. By 1927 there had been a proposal to close Eldon and Chilton. Fortunately, both pits survived that crisis. Even so, in April 1930, Chilton Colliery was described as follows, in hardly complimentary terms.

Chilton, showing Durham Road taken in the early 1930s.

The Star Picture Hall *is first on the left followed in order by **Richardson's Chemists, Hanna Parker's Fish Shop, Thompson's Fruit and Veg.** (now the Post Office), **Pawson's Cafe and Liddle's Shoe Shop**.Mr. Liddle, a cobbler by trade did shoe repair) in a small workshop to the rear of Durham Road. A little further on, opposite the club entrance, is **Walter Wilsons (grocers)**, opened on 16th July 1928 and closed January 25th 1985.*
The West Cornforth Ind. Co-op. Soc. *commenced business in 1921 and closed 27th December 1969. They occupied the premises which is now **Multifit/Durham Design**, the shop on the corner was **Harry Barker's (grocers)** Durham Road branch.*

"On the whole, the colliery has a shabby and unkempt look and the heapsteads, screens, etc. (the surface area in general) is in a dirty and unkempt condition."

Eldon Colliery, with many years of high coal production behind it, was now working the last of its profitable coal reserves. Difficulties would arise, profit margins would slump, to say nothing of the cost of pumping an ever-increasing amount of water to the surface. Current market forces were unfavourable, with economic gloom on the horizon. All of these were against the mine staying open. It was no surprise to some, but a shock to many, when a notice was posted on 6th June 1931, by the Eldon Mineral Estates Records, stating that, "Eldon was closed down and it was not known if she would reopen." Eldon did not reopen; it was only a matter of time before they would shut down the pumps at the shaft bottom.

When that fateful day came, it was in the certain knowledge that Chilton and the workings at the Windlestone end of the pit would be doomed to flooding, with closure inevitable along with Eldon. All three pits were linked together underground.

Pumping did cease at Eldon and the water began to rise in all three connected pits. It was nothing short of a disaster. Coal mining at Chilton and Windlestone came to an abrupt halt before anyone had time to draw breath, bringing about one of the bleakest periods the miners and their families would have to face. Pease and Partners' long association with the village was at an end. The legacy of Eldon Colliery had finally arrived.

Look for a Silver Lining

This song, popular during the First World War 1914-18, had words that could not have been better written, nor more suited, to the men, women and children of our community whose continuing saga of struggle and strife seemed to have no end. The words and music have a quality which, on occasion, can uplift those who are down and raise the spirits of those, to whom fate has dealt, once again, another a cruel blow. Very apt for our residents, who needed something after receiving another kick in the teeth, as the saying goes.

Look for a silver lining, whene're the sun appears in the blue;
You know that somewhere the sun is shining,
and so the right thing to do, is make it shine for you;
A heart full of song and gladness,
will always banish sorrow and strife;
So always look for a silver lining,
and try to find the sunny side of life.

The focal point of any mine is the headgear and pulley wheels.

The pit headgear on the main shaft is seen crashing to the ground. The date, 2/8/1933, and the time, 3.25pm.

For the inhabitants of Chilton and Windlestone, the beginning of the 1930s was, unfortunately, a continuation, and even a worsening, of the conditions in the 1920s. Poaching and stealing were a necessity for survival, although the situation did improve, albeit gradually.

Putting on a Brave Face

The situation facing Chilton in 1931, and the outlook for the foreseeable future seemed very bleak indeed. There were grave economic problems facing the whole of the UK bringing suffering and hardship, with unemployment rising from 1,336,000 in November 1929 to 2.5 million in December 1930. Conditions did not improve again until 1932, when a gradual recovery of world trade took place. Unemployment climbed as high as 36.5%, being the highest in those areas such as Wales and Northern England where the heavy industries were most common.

An extract from the Council Minutes Book, July 14th 1931, showed the rateable value of the township had decreased from near £3600 in 1914 to £2756 in 1930 and there would be a "further reduction seeing that Messrs. Pease and Partners were abandoning both Chilton and Windlestone Collieries."

Putting on a brave face was all anyone could do; thank goodness it cost nothing.

Unemployment in Durham was spread over a much longer period than most other areas of the country and was much more intense. The population declined as young men and women moved south in search of work. Coal production in the Auckland district had fallen from 1929 to 1932, but it began to rise as the economy improved. Chilton's closure had become much more serious than the position of some of her neighbours, since the mine was closed completely and when other pits began to recover in 1933, only five men were employed by Pease and Partners at Chilton, repairing cottages.

Our residents needed no reminding of the plight facing them, but when fate is working overtime it does the job properly; and so it would be a silent crowd who witnessed the demolition of Windlestone Colliery surface buildings in 1933. Gus Pettigeen, I am told, was originally from Belgium. He was an accomplished miner and was in charge of rasing all the surface buildings to the ground, after working there for many years.

Ashes to Ashes and Dust to Dust.

Swings and Roundabouts

You know what they say about swings and roundabouts: one hopes events might go full circle and, maybe, could pick up where they left off and carry on as before. The hope men and women shared in Chilton in 1931 was, it's happened before, the pit shut down, then it re-opened. Could it happen again? Would the cycle be repeated? Mining folk were ever the optimists, hoping against hope that something would turn up. However, there would be others, they would be saying, "I think we've had it this time" and who could blame them? After all,

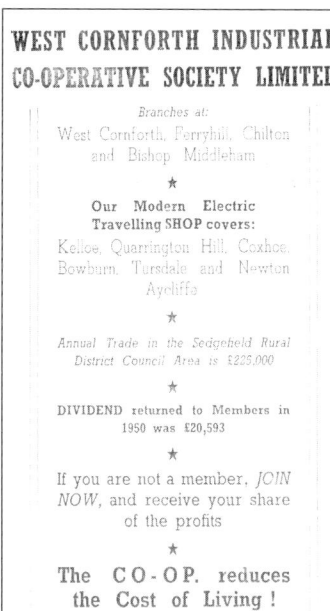

the pit was flooded with the water well up the shafts at Chilton by this time.

It was inevitable that the village population would decline, with miners finding work elsewhere and taking their families with them. School attendances took another tumble, no one was surprised. In 1932 there were 692 children attending school and by 1936 this figure had fallen to 531.

With the demise of Pease and Partners in the village, it was no surprise when, in 1933, the Council were offered, and accepted the gift of the recreation grounds, and took over all the responsibilities and liabilities from January 1st.

Chilton Pit, back from its watery grave for another 32 years drawn by the author

Chilton Buildings looking north about 1934. The first house on the left at this time belonged to Dr. Mathew Hunter. His surgery was the single storey building to the rear and is still there to this day. Further on is the post office run by Mr. and Mrs. Charlton. It also boasted a lending library, the librarian being Linda Pettigeen. Linda eventually married and took over the post office, when it transferred to its present day site in Durham Road. The Union Room follows, used to collect union subscriptions from the miners, and for Chilton Colliery Band practice. Next door, The Wheatsheaf public house.

With the Council now in control of the recreation grounds, they began to replace the mine owners as the dominant influence in the village. In 1933, rumour had it that the pit might reopen, by September. It was a fact, the doubters were to be proved wrong and the faithful, hoping against hope, got their pit back. The swings and roundabouts theory had, once again, come up trumps. This time the saviour was Dorman and Long, Steelmasters of Teesside. The pit shafts at the mine had been sealed for safety reasons, so it was a small, expectant group of miners who were given the initial task, on 1st September 1933, of breaking into the top of No. 1 Pit to remove the seal. The first men involved here were W. Dobson and J. Atkinson. At the No. 2 Pit, a start was made ten days later, with the first men breaking in there being W. Rodgers, G. Oliver and J. Robinson (Fiddler).

The aim of the new owners was, naturally, to commence production as soon as was practicable, working the Five Quarter and Main Coal seams, lying at a much-reduced depth from the surface than the mining operations of the previous 30 years under Stobart and Pease. The old enemy, water was the first priority, having been allowed to rise while the mine was closed. It was just below the Three Quarter seam, a metre 365 feet, from the surface. In the circumstances, the mine and the village were indeed fortunate to get another chance.

In the second half of 1934, Dorman and Long were employing 149 men as new roadways were developed giving greater access to the coal seam. So it was that production increased and more miners were set on, with 928 on the books by 1937.

Even so, this was nowhere near the employment levels of the 1920s and, although it was an improvement, the situation could not be regarded as a return to normal.

The Council continued their activities throughout this period, although restricted by the effects of the Depression. They continually pursued a request for more bus services in the

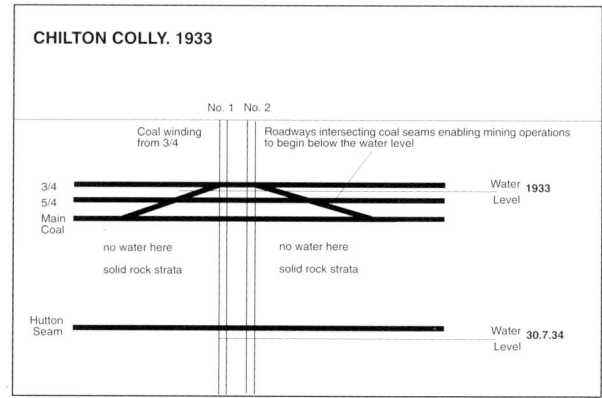

This diagram illustrates how the mining engineers of the day got round the problem of the high water level. By driving inclined roadways (drifts), through solid rock until they reached the coal seams a safe distance from the water in the pit shafts, then winding the coal from the 3/4 seam level, a few feet above the water.

region, stimulated by the need of many men in the area who were travelling to work, and, incidentally, they did not want to lose residents to other communities if it could be avoided. In 1935, Pease and Partners sold the allotment land to the local authority.

On the Lighter Side

The saying "all work and no play, makes Jack a dull boy" applies equally to both men and women. I have said much of the struggle and strife, but there was indeed a lighter side to the people of Chilton and Windlestone.

In 1932, an "aged people's treat" was organised, and may well have been done by the Workmen's Club, something they were very good at for many years. 1933 saw Spennymoor Brass Band playing in the recreation ground with a collection held in aid of the band's funds. These events, and many others, highlighted a change in atmosphere in the village, with residents becoming more leisure-conscious.

Throughout the following years, Chilton had a bowling club, cricket club, and a junior and senior football club in all the local leagues. In conjunction with these clubs, other forms of entertainment were organised each week to make money. One example:

"That the use of the Tennis Pavilion be granted for Whist Drives, every Wednesday evening, on the same terms as last year." (Bowling Club request to the Council 1935.)

The Council provided tennis rackets and balls so that everyone had the opportunity to play the game. A sports committee continued to organise an annual sports day and, in 1937, the manager of the mine was interviewed by the Council:

"In respect to the games of the inter-colliery competitions for cricket, bowls and tennis, he wished to play in the Recreation Ground."

A "Chilton and Windlestone girls' club for sport" was organised, and they were granted the use of the football pitch for exercises.

Mainsforth miners' lodge proposed the building of a swimming pool in the area. Chilton council seriously considered this, until the idea had to be abandoned due to the threat of the Second World War looming onto the horizon.

In 1936, another milestone was reached relating to leisure, and that was the grand opening of the Regal Cinema, now Ken Warne's supermarket. Dr. Mathew Hunter was given the honour of declaring the cinema open on Monday 3rd June l936 at 5.30pm. The handbill for that occasion makes interesting reading.

1937 saw the Workingmen's Club move into new premises. There appeared to be no expense spared, with spacious rooms and comfortable seating. This along with the new cinema was evidence of prosperity and advancement. Many would feel that the village was headed in the right direction.

REGAL CINEMA
CHILTON BUILDINGS.

The Opening of the above Cinema by Dr. M. Hunter on Monday, June 8th, 1936, at 5-30 p.m.

Mon., Tues. & Wed., June 8th, 9th & 10th,
ROBERT DONAT & MADELEINE CARROLL, in

THE 39 STEPS

Monday—TWO HOUSES—commence at 6-15 & 8-30 p.m.
Tuesday & Wednesday—Only ONE House—commence at 7-15 p.m.

Thurs., Fri & Sat, June 11th 12th & 13th,
JESSIE MATTHEWS with SONNIE HALE, in

FIRST A GIRL

Another Musical Comedy.

SUNDAY, June 14th,
Leslie Fuller, in "LOST IN THE LEGION,"
also All-Star Cast in
"MY SONG GOES ROUND THE WORLD."

Next Week; "Cock o' the North,' "Father O'Flynn."

Prices: BALCONY, 9d.; PIT, 6d; CHILDREN, 3d.

Wearmouth & Jones, Spennymoor.   Children must be paid for.

The development of new interests led to the neglect of others. In 1936 the council agreed to "accept the gift of a billiard table, library and furniture belonging to the Chilton Institute now closed owing to the lack of interest shown in providing another institute."

After the glory days of the 1920s it was a sad day, and hard to believe that the football team ,Chilton RA should have financial problems. The new interests and activities were drawing away would-be spectators from their games. From 1935 they were continually in arrears with their ground rent, with the Council finally engaging a solicitor to deal with the matter by 1938.

Education

In areas such as Chilton, with low wages and large families, it meant a great sacrifice for the whole family to send one child for further education and, to the majority of people, it seemed an unnecessary effort.

Not that there was much of an option, for most young men felt obliged to earn a living, and followed their fathers into the mines. Unlike those new areas in the county where light engineering had established itself, there was little opportunity at Chilton for a technical career. Anyone with ambition other than mining had to leave the district.

Towards World War Two

So it was, by 1939, with the Second World War looming onto the horizon, there had developed a village very different from that of 1900. The Lord of the Manor and his influence had disappeared, to be replaced by the authority of the "Council" who now represented the people's interests.

Chilton entered the war with a 70-year history of mining and hardship, with a determination and a will to win being second nature to its residents. With this kind of spirit prevailing, one looked to the future knowing there would be change and sacrifices to make, but with hope also that they would eventually win through.

Amy Johnson

Amy Johnson was born on 1st July 1903 in Kingston- upon-Hull. She belonged to an elite group of pioneering aviators,who,during the 1920s and 30s, flew single-engined light aircraft.The purpose,to test the machines and, at the same time their own endurance and stamina.These flights were, in many cases, the forerunner to regular air routes around the globe.

It was no mean feat to sit in one of these small aircraft for hours on end, taking whatever Mother Nature had to offer. There would be fine weather and plenty of the other. Rain, fog and cold would be part of it, the burdens of fatigue and loneliness, at times, being a price Amy would have to pay for her fame. From May 5th to 24th 1930, she flew a De Havilland Gipsy Moth named Jason from England to Australia, solo, creating a record and winning £10,000.

The world applauded Miss Amy Johnson after completing her record solo flight in under three weeks. Amy is seen here acknowledging the cheers of the crowds on her arrival in Sydney.

The inset is of her Gipsy Moth flying over Port Darwin on 24th May.

From July 25th to August 6th 1931, she flew a De Havilland Puss Moth from England to Tokyo, Japan. In 1932 she married Jim Mollison, a Scotsman and pioneer aviator.

You may wonder what this has to do with Chilton. In November 1930, a plane was spotted by a group of boys playing at the west end of Raby Terrace. One of those boys, **Fred Thompson**, now living in 13 Jade Walk, lived in Raby Terrace at that time, and remembers the day, even though he was only 6 years old. "I remember it was silver in colour. The weather was bad and the plane came down in the long field next to the Plantation Wood. Some of the older boys made a grab at the tail of the plane as it came to a stop. The young woman who alighted from the cockpit was none other than the world-famous flyer Amy Johnson.

She had been flying north to Scotland to see her fiance, Jim Mollison, the bad weather forcing her to make an unscheduled stop, short of fuel. This picture, previously unpublished, shows Amy Johnson's plane, down in the field near to Plantation Wood on

what appears to be a wet day, judging by the clothing of those gathered around. Three policemen are on hand to look after the De Havilland Puss Moth, a relatively new aircraft, the first flight of this type being in May 1930. The husband of the lady on the left with the umbrella took this photo.

Kathleen Oates now lives in Charlotte Terrace and also remembers the day. "We lived in 8 New South View and my father had the petrol station at the top of Rushyford Bank, where

Oates Garage as Amy Johnson would have seen it in 1930, seven years before the new Club was built, allowing us to see the two chimneys of Chilton Colliery in the background. The man having his picture taken is Bob Oates, the proprietor.

Vine Place is now. There was a knock at the door which father answered. He was informed that a plane had landed to the rear of the garage, and that it was Amy Johnson, the famous flyer, asking if he would refuel her plane. I remember that my younger brother, Allen, was in the bath and only a year old. He was dried quickly, a blanket wrapped round him, and we all went to the garage. There was a large crowd gathered round the plane and I am almost certain that father filled the plane's petrol tank."

Billy Davidson lives in Dene Bridge Row, now in his 80s he was just a mere boy, and remembers the event as if it were yesterday.

"When the plane landed, there was soon a crowd surrounding her as she alighted. Amy was wearing a leather flying jacket and trousers, together with her hat and goggles. Everyone wanted to help her, including Fred Allison (Codger). He asked if he could carry her bag, but she declined. Instead, she said she, almost out of fuel, and would someone kindly let the garage know, it being only a short distance away?

Amy Johnson flew out of Chilton the next day, one presumes north, to Scotland. No doubt she would get a good send off, wishing her a safe journey. On 20th May 1940, Amy Johnson joined the Air Transport Auxiliary attached to the Royal Air Force, delivering new aircraft to bomber and fighter stations throughout the British Isles.

On 5th January 1941, Amy was flying an Air Speed Oxford twin-engined aircraft 3540 for delivery to Kidlington, Oxfordshire. Taking off from Squires Gate Airfield at Blackpool at 11.49 am, by 15.54 hours she was approaching the 952 Thames Barrage Naval Squadron and was in difficulties, parachuting from her aircraft into Hearne Bay near Margate. The naval ship HMS Haslemere was on patrol in Hearne Bay and saw her parachute into the sea. The Lt. Commander of the ship, 34-year-old Walter Fletcher, dived in to save her, but they both lost their lives. His body was recovered, but Amy's body was never found. She was only 37 years old.

Famous aviator Amy Johnson, a legend in her lifetime

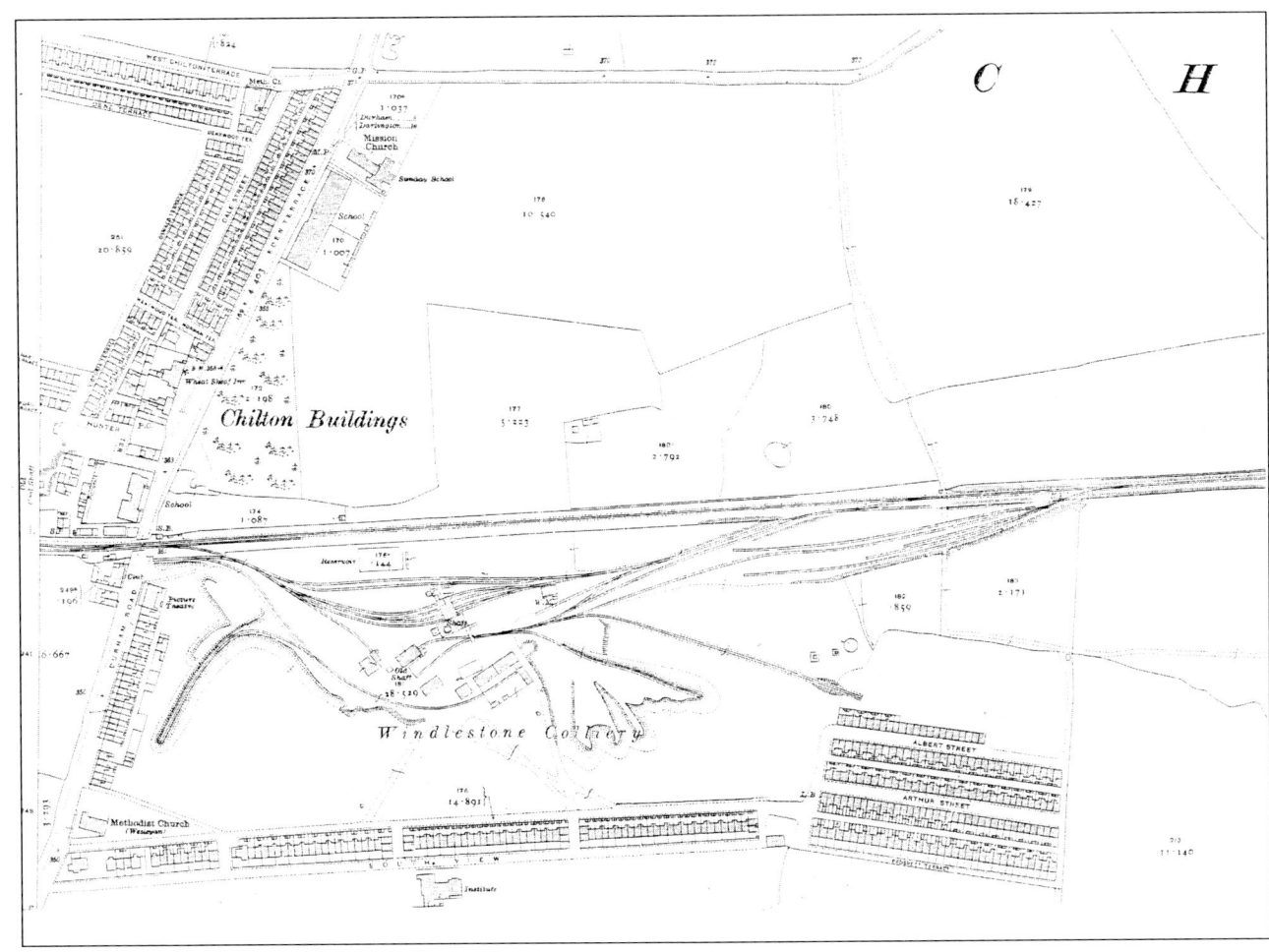

*Windlestone Colliery in 1919, when
the pit was at its peak.*

*An increase in the number of railway
sidings to cope with larger tonnages
of coal, and an increase in miners'
houses, was a sign of those times.*

CHAPTER EIGHT

The War Years
1939-45

The War Years 1939-45

One thing the war did almost at a stroke was to reduce unemployment. Men and women were involved in anything and everything which would further our chances of winning the war against Germany. For the most part,children were untouched by the rigours and horror of war; they still played, went to school and a great many went to church or chapel. As far as they were concerned, the war may well have been on another planet.

Those who were at home did their utmost to support the men fighting for them in the Armed Forces. Coal production at the mine increased and as a consequence more miners were employed. With every ton of coal needed,country-wide, to raise steam for power stations, the locomotives on the railways, who in turn were themselves moving coal to where it was needed - most aspects of manufacturing industry, to say nothing of domestic heating and cooking,all relied on coal. Aand what of the Royal and Merchant Navies, which were powered by steam engines. All this made the miner's role vital.

An industry constantly under pressure was the Ordinance Factories making ammunition, one such factory being sited on land now occupied by Aycliffe Industrial Estate. With the men away fighting a war, and the pits taking every man they could get hold of, the women were left to do this most dangerous of work, risking their lives daily, making bullets and shells twenty-four hours a day, with enemy planes doing their utmost to locate the site and destroy it. These brave women of all ages acquired a very apt name, Angels of the North. They were recognised for their crucial contribution, rightly so, but it took almost 60 years.

Items, from waste paper and tin cans, to jam jars, anything! that would recycle was collected and used again in some form or another. All this came under the general heading "The War Effort". Periodically, the Regal Cinema would hold a Saturday afternoon children's matinee, and the price of admission was two or three dozen jam jars or a pile of newspapers or magazines. They were collected by children going from door to door with the response from residents guaranteed. They saved everything they could spare for each collection.

Moving coal gave the railways something to think about

This snap of the Regal Cinema shortly after closure, 1960s

Childhood Memories

I was five years old when war broke out in 1939. With two brothers, Norman aged seven and Peter, one, we lived with Mum and Dad in New South View, Windlestone. The Chilton Board School being the start of my education, I went at seven, on to Chilton Council School at the top of the village.

Free milk was delivered in third and half pint pint bottles. They had cardboard inserts in the top of.the bottle, the middle you pressed in to insert your straw.Each classroom had a large, cast iron fireplace; on cold, frosty mornings it would be lit and burning brightly when the bell went to summon us to our lessons. A large coal scuttle was at hand to keep the fire going. In addition, a double row of hot-water pipes encircled the classroom, bringing extra heat from the boiler house.

Rules and Regulations

Chilton, like anywhere else in the country, was subject to a multitude of regulations brought in for everyone's safety in the likelihood of an air raid. A complete blackout was enforced by the local Civil Defence combined with the Air Raid Precautions Unit (ARP), with men drawn from the community to work day or night, usually fitting in with their full-time work and allowing them to be available if the air raid siren went off.

As children we were carried downstairs, mostly still asleep, and I laid gently in the cupboard under the stairs, on a shakey-down (a bed made up) on the floor. It was deemed the safest place should the house suffer a hit. Our dad would don his tin helmet and greatcoat, go on duty, checking for any chinks of light, and generally being at the ready in case of trouble, staying out until the "all clear" was sounded. He would then go off to Fishburn Pit, many times with very little sleep. He was not alone. The ARP station was situated in the building which forms the front of our present day Medical Centre.

County  of Durham

CIVIL DEFENCE GENERAL SERVICES

In the years when our country was in mortal danger *H. Turner* who served in the Civil Defence *Wardens* Service gave generously of h*is* time and powers to bring relief and comfort to those who suffered the misfortune of enemy air attack.

R. S. M. Middlewood.

CHAIRMAN OF THE COUNTY EMERGENCY COMMITTEE.

J. Cittoke

COUNTY A.R.P. CONTROLLER.

31ST JULY, 1945.

The Blackout

Houses were equipped with blackout roller blinds and the windows were fitted with broad strips of adhesive tape in a diamond pattern, to minimise flying glass in the event of a bomb blast. Transport of all types drove through the blackout, moving essential supplies and workers, keeping to their schedules, hardly able to see where they were going in the dark.

The Royal Air Force had trailers designed to carry their Spitfire and Hurricane fighter aircraft by road. They came through Chilton, the fuselage on one trailer followed by the wings on another.

Situated on the Great North Road, before motorways had been thought of, all military traffic on the east side of the country lumbered through our village. Massive tank and heavy gun carriers, smaller tanks in convoy would go through, often with one of the crew on observation duty, standing up with the hatch cover back, impressions never to be forgotten by a young boy.

Oates' Garage was commandeered by the Army, with their convoys of vehicles filling up there, with the odd civilian transport who needed petrol coupons to purchase fuel.

Windlestone Colly. Institute housed a good number of Army personnel in the main hall.Beds and belongings were arranged along each side, much like a dormitory.

The Manor House/Eden Arms was occupied by American troops at one stage of the war, bringing with them chocolates, cigarettes and nylons. All were very scarce; needless-to-say, they got plenty of visitors - men, women and children.

Windlestone Hall was home to 150 German women taken prisoner by British forces. It was known that German officers were allowed to sleep in the Hall while British staff stayed in the barn. Marjorie Heather Gracie was the only woman allowed to head such a camp. She spoke of the problems of handling Germans who had been brainwashed into believing they were superior to their enemies, causing problems with discipline. Violence in these camps was prevalent. I only ever saw German male officers being

All military traffic on the east side of the country rolled through the village

Wagons rolled through Chilton in the blackout.

marched down the road on Sunday from the Hall to St Aidan's for morning service, and working on the farms. Chilton railway crossing used to be a daily bottle-neck. Morning and evening, the amount of traffic using the road could be held up as far as the cemetery one way, and back to Rushyford the other. Coal trains passed over regularly with up to 40 twenty ton trucks. The queue was aggravated by the number of buses in use carrying employees to their work at Aycliffe Munitions Factory.

School children were required to carry gas masks in a cardboard box with a strap to go over the shoulder. Everyone was shown how to use the mask in the event of an air raid.

At the sound of a continuous bell ringing, lessons ceased immediately. Gas masks were picked up and sometimes worn, and we evacuated school in an orderly procession, smaller children going first, across the school yard to a concrete shelter. This was our air raid practice.

The headmaster, Mr.Ross, was six feet tall, ramrod straight, and often wore a dark-blue, pin stripe suit. He was very strict but we liked him. Twice a week he would take the class and continue to read a story to us, then ask questions about it. Treasure Island by R. L. Stevenson is one I remember to this day. He could transport a young mind back in time to conjure up this Island better than any modern-day television set. Mr. Ross could be seen, along with other teachers, walking down the main street, walking-stick in hand, looking more like an army captain than a teacher, in order to catch the United bus which arrived at 4.55pm for Durham where he lived. Sadly, he died in my last year at school in 1949. I attended his memorial service in St.Aidan's with the rest of my year. He would be about 55.

There were many strange young faces in class at this time. They were evacuees, moved for their own safety from cities and towns suffering heavy aerial bombardment in the Midlands and the South. Two boys stayed at our home, from Southampton, their names, Jim and Reg Whickham. A number of homes had a soldier assigned for his meals; ours was Hugh Gibson from Chelmsford. His people were farmers and for many years after the war we received a box of apples in the autumn.

Evacuees with their gas masks. Some arrived in Chilton

Jack Kell in familiar pose

Jack Kell - Blacksmith

As a young man, his forge was in the blacksmith's shop at Rushyford. With the sale of the Eden Estate in 1936, he was given the chance to bid for a piece of land in Chilton to the rear of the Board School, not far off Mason's pit shaft. Although not filled in, it was surrounded by a wall to keep mischievous children, dogs and cats out. The local business people who made housecalls used traps and carts for deliveries of milk, fresh fruit and veg. The farmer's equipment, such as the plough, harrow and rake, were all horse-drawn, making Jack Kell a very busy man. There were always horses stood waiting to be shoed, when we as boys used to stand and watch, totally absorbed. The white-hot flames of the forge, the clanging of his hammer on steel, making shoes, the amazement when Jack would lift a leg of one of these great animals and put it between his own. Using a file, rasp and cutting knife to trim overgrown hooves, and with the shoe still glowing red, he would firmly place it on the horse's hoof. The burning smell I can never forget to this day and, miraculously, the horse never moved. Jack won many farrier competitions, had lots of trophies and was highly respected in his trade.

He may have been busy man, but he also found time to be officer in charge of the Home Guard in Chilton.

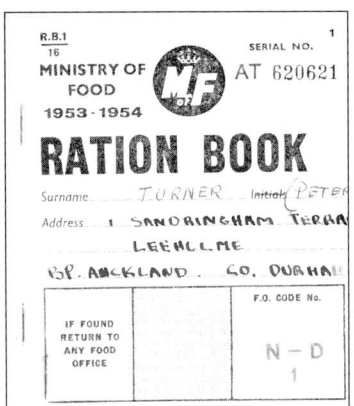

The Home Guard

Formerly the Local Defence Volunteers (LDV), they had their headquarters in the Bandroom next to the Wheatsheaf and were split into sections to keep watch on the main road through the village. A practice firing range, with butts, was situated on Chilton pit heap, 300 yards long, stretching near to the hedge on the Kirk Merrington road. Weapons issued were 303 rifles and Sten guns. A Major Guthrie MC was Commanding Officer.

Chilton Colly had its own section, Sgt. Bill Lamb in command, of 49 West Chilton Terrace It numbered 16: the Stubbs of l0 Norman Terrace, Pte. Thomas of 1 Woodham View, Pte. McKenna of l0 Keats Road, to name but a few.

A searchlight station, located along Chilton Lane on the right side of the road, opposite the former vicarage, was manned by regular soldiers and, later, by American personnel. The Home Guard had training sessions with the regulars; they arranged a match on the firing range at the pit, the Home Guard won.

Rationing

During the war years, and for a time after, most items of food and clothing were rationed. Each person was issued with a ration book of coupons, allowing purchase of a limited amount of goods. Butter, tea, margarine, sugar, meat, sweets and clothes were all rationed. I remember butter being two ounces per person, whatever there was being only enough to get by, and if we moaned, our parents were quick to say, " Think yourselves very lucky. Ships bringing food into the country are running the risk of being hit by torpedoes from German submarines to feed us all."

Nothing was wasted. The "tattee peelins" etc. went to the allotments or gardens to feed hens, ducks, rabbits or pigeons. Anything to make a meal, using any spare land for vegetables and in most instances where a swap could be done, veg was exchanged for eggs and suchlike, a real garden economy with very little money changing hands.

Black-leaded Fireplaces, Tin Baths and Clippy Mats

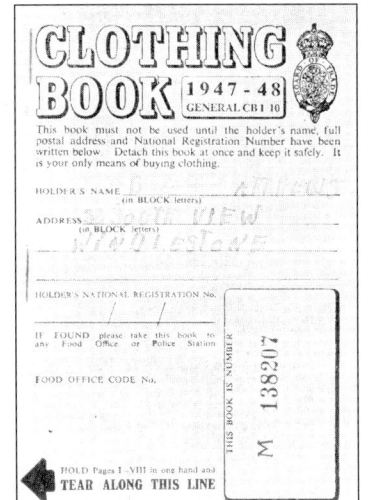

During the 1940s, the black cast iron fireplace was still the most important piece of equipment in the home. The majority of men working in the village were miners, arriving home at all the odd hours of the day and night, due to shiftwork,looking as black as the coal seams they were working in. Part of these monstrous fireplaces housed a side boiler full of hot water, heated from a fire that rarely went out. The boiler was constantly being emptied to fill the zinc-covered tin bath brought in from the back yard where it usually hung on a six-inch nail knocked into the backyard wall.

In earlier times, and probably as late as the 1930s, where the father and two or three sons were in the same household, all working at the pit, it was not uncommon for the wife and mother to sit up all night, dozing in her rocking chair. She would be waiting to call someone up for work, starting at 3am (foreshift). After seeing him off to the pit, she would then wait of another coming in off nightshift at 6 or 7am ensuring there was hot water, using a ladling tin to fill his bath, as well as having a bite to eat on the table before going to bed.

A black-leaded fireplace,oven left, side boiler right, and a clippy mat in its frame in the process of being made.

When we were small we could get in the bath, one lot of hot water had to do for all of us. When our dad came in from work, he sat on a cracket (stool) beside the bath to wash his feet. As we got older, we knelt on a towel beside the bath. There was a bonus, we got dried beside a big hot fire. Our dad had 16 bags of concessionary coal from the pit every 28 days, the fire always blazing away during the winter days keeping us warm, giving a sense of security and comfort to us kids sat in its glow with our parents on dark nights, listening to the wireless, reading a comic or playing games. The coal oven had the fire banked up against it to have it hot enough to bake. Mum would test the oven's heat by opening the door and putting her hand in for a few moments. Judging by the results of her cooking, we scoffed the lot,was testimony to her methods.The kettle, pans and cooking pot were all cast iron, staying in the family sometimes for generations. All veg, bacon and eggs were done on the fire, Sunday dinner with Yorkshire puddings and cakes for tea, as good as any you might have today.

On Sundays, the front room fire was lit. Mum and dad would sit in there with their feet up with the Sunday paper or a library book from the old post office run by Mr. and Mrs Charlton, Linda Pettijeen being the librarian.

Clippy mats were in evidence all over the house. They were made in the house using jute (sackcloth), tacked to a wooden frame and stretched on two flat pieces of wood with a series

Baking using the coal oven

of holes drilled in to take pegs. All items of worn clothing were put into a sack, until there was a clippy mat session. Any members of the family with a bit of spare time would cut strips of clothing or do some of the mat. Sometimes four of them sat on chairs, talking away and using a prodding hook (prodder), pushing the hook through the jute and pulling a strip of clothing up and through to form a loop, following a pattern drawn previously, squares, diamonds or a flower design. They all looked nice when completed,the main thing being, it was cheap and hard-wearing. There was still very little money about in the 1940s, with clippy mats to be seen in many homes in the 1950s.

The Star Picture Hall, closed since 1936, became a fire station during the war. Occupied by the Auxiliary Fire Service (AFS), they were the local back-up in the event of bombing. Sandy Matthews, a short thick-set man from the Windlestone streets, was in charge. The audience seats were taken out, revealing the sloping floor, the screen was left in place, and a small hut constructed, acting as an office. Among the assortment of equipment used were two large vans, altered for use as fire engines and painted dark blue.

Our Adventure Playground

As children, we played mostly outside, summer and winter, the derelict site of Windlestone pit being the finest adventure playground one could hope for. An old reservoir near the railway had about 3 feet of water in it and it was home to frogs, newts, larve and small lizards, up

Our adventure playground, the pit heap and ruins of Windlestone Colly with a load of concessionary coal tipped at the rear of South View.Many's the time we went round shoveling it into the coal house at 6d (2.5p) a time.

The 40s, 50s and 60s

Getting Back to Normal

With the war over in 1945, men and women were demobilised from the armed forces, a steady stream returning back to their homes, Chilton no different to other towns and villages. Some had been away since 1939, others, never to return, the unlucky ones, buried in the killing fields of Europe. Let us not forget also the civilian casualties incurred by constant bombardment on our own soil. They paid the ultimate sacrifice for the safety and freedom of families they held dear to them.

For those who survived, they were all heroes, bunting tied to lamposts, parties and "Welcome Home" dances at the Club, and street parties all part of the celebrations. There were those who needed time to readjust after the trauma of war. These brave people slowly but surely filtered back to their jobs and family life.

Chilton Girls School 1949. **back row l. to r:** *Shirley Patterson, Doreen Jackson, Elsie Mudd, Pearl Hutchinson, Mary Allison, Christina Pearson, Dorothea Horn, Edna Thompson, Mary Williams.* **middle row:** *Margaret Nobbs, Thelma Dobson, Marie Moses, Betty Hopper, Beryl Matthews, Sheila Duffy, Prunella Gowland, Greta Redden, Brenda Raine, Peggy Robinson, Miss Hope (teacher).* **front row:** *Margaret Vickers, Norma Thompson, June Eliott, Sheila McConnel, Sylvia Swainston, Sylvia Murray, Jean Wilkinson, Hazel Thompson, Margaret James, Doreen Hockworth.*

Women's Institute football team 1950s
standing, l to r: *Mrs.Wilson,*
Mrs. Clennald, Darby (club), Betty ?,
?, (Potts P.C's wife), Buckle, Hannah
Parker. **kneeling:** *Pearson, Eva*
Sewell, ?, Connie Parker, Marshall.

The local branch of the Women's Institute,well supported, have organised a great many functions over the years. Mrs. Sewell, now aged 94, remembers well her time in the 1950s. Christmas parties for themselves and the children, outings, and football matches played against Chilton Club.

The Opposition
standing l to r: *?, ?, Ray Bradshaw,*
Potts (P.C.), Marshall, Tom Bradshaw.
kneeling: *Longstaffe, H. Foster, John*
Payton.

Progress

The war had a great effect on the village and the miners. The ammunition factory closed down at Aycliffe and out of its ashes has arisen the modern Industrial Estate we see today, with dozens of estates in the embryo stage springing up all over the area. Light engineering took over from the manufacture of bullets and shells, these firms offering an alternative to mining for both men and women. Boys with ability were encouraged by their fathers and teachers to take skilled work in the factories.

With apprenticeships being offered in mechanical and electrical trades, these young people matured to form a new type of class within the mining community, their contribution to society being a change of values and opinions differing from the traditions of previous years.

Women were no longer tied to the home with little or no prospects. Their efforts in all spheres of industry and agriculture during wartime had given them a chance to earn a living, in many cases, side by side with the men, bringing independence, respect and their own money. Mining tradition and the old ways, where the man had been dominating affairs for so long, were slow to vanish, but the women had money to spend. With the single lady it was clothes and stockings, the married women tended to channel their new-found wealth into the home, with furniture and fittings improving their quality of life and young members of the family having the opportunity of entering college or university.

A Return to the Pit

Chilton Pit, for all its ups and downs, still had the honour of being the main employer. Coal production in the 1940's and 50's was the highest in the pit's history, with conveyor belts starting to replace the haulage engines and the ponies. The number of men employed underground was 1150, with 303 on the surface, and a weekly output in excess of 9000 tons, some of this from the Hutton seam. Old habits and a way of life still preserved, even in the face of progress. Miners who knew no other work were reluctant to change; so long as the pit was there, so were they.

In 1947, the mine became state owned, heralding the era of the National Coal Board (NCB) subsequently British Coal. Dorman and Long, the previous owners, were now history. Almost at a stroke, the pressure to make profits before safety were eased and slowly but surely, the safety of workers was paramount under the NCB Chilton was now part of No. 4 Area, Durham Divisional Coal Board, with their headquarters at Green Lane, Spennymoor, now the Administration Centre for Sedgefield Borough Council

For the miner, conditions did improve, but there were still accidents. On occasion the roof

Darlington Road, the Band Room, Post Office, Hutton House and the Old Board School 1950.

The coal face, pretty much how it was at Chilton in the 1940s and 50s. For the purist this is a 25hp British Jeffrey Diamond face conveyor drive, with the roof supported by Dowty hydraulic props.

above the coal could cave in and trap someone; a miner may walk into a roadway that is poorly ventilated, devoid of life supporting oxygen, replaced by a gas named blackdamp. It has no smell and is fatal to the unsuspecting man who does not quickly step back into fresh air.

Firedamp, no smell, it is the unrefined form of the gas we use in our kitchens, commonly known as methane. Explosive, given the proper quantities of gas and air mixed, all it takes is a spark. Seeping out of the coal as it does, it requires a good air current to dilute it and render it harmless. Mechanical accidents being another hazard, waiting for the miner who is not alert or gets careless.

Unfortunately, mining is a risky business, a fact accepted by all those who work in the industry, and fatal accidents do occur. In earlier times, it was not uncommon for the woman to become head of the household, her status, Widow, as can be seen from the census form of 1891 in Windlestone. The combined list of fatal accidents at both pits is a long one. However, it would be remiss of me not to mention some of those who gave their lives trying to make an honest living to keep a wife and raise a family.

Killed at Chilton since 1936		
Mr. Walker	Putter	24/9/36
J. Bails	Putter	31/12/36
T. Longstaff	Bargain Work	30/1/37
Mr. Thorburn	Putter	15/8/39
A. Stott	Onsetter	3/4/40
J. Orange	Hewer	21/5/43
W. Close	Hewer	27/4/44
R. Carter	Hewer	9/4/45
W. Ratcliffe	Piece Work	28/5/47
Mr. Foster	Piece Work	28/5/47
Mr. Thompson	Hewer	26/11/47
Mr. Ibottson	Wagon way	13/2/48
F. Hodgon		/5/50
W. Christon	Coal Cutter	18/5/50
L. Coates (in the pit yard)		17/7/50
M. Smith	Deputy	9/7/56
K. Denham	Face Worker	9/12/58

The census shows this widow (as marked) became the head of her household

Working under the Main Gate Caunch, a high-risk area where the face conveyor feeds onto a chain conveyor and explained visually in the next photo

The pit did well on its own. Only when the decision was made to couple up to Dean and Chapter, at Ferryhill and Leasingthorne, which was completed by December 1960, did the rot set in. As events subsequently proved, this combined mine became a loss-maker.

The caunch (canch) is the rock above the seam in the main gate, blasted down each day to make way for the arch girders supporting the roadway. The chain conveyor on the right taking the coal away, and, finally, a miner's lamp hung on the left, if needed.

A Little Nostalgia

Some black faces here. Above, a group of officials (Overmen) in Chilton pit yard about 1954, some going on shift, others just finished.

standing, l to r:

Kit Nicholson (Eden Terr.), Tommy Briggs and Ernie Williams (Leeholme), Teddy Thompson and Teddy Pearson (Chilton), Tom Owens (Merrington). **kneeling, l to r:** *George Brewis (Leeholme), Jack Sumpton (Merrington), Stan Johnson.*

The obsolete coke ovens chimney coming down in 1948 with No. 1 Pit pulley wheels in the background

*Unwinding worn strand, Chilton aerial flight 1954, **l to r:** Norman Winter, Fred Thompson.*

*Under-Officials' and Engineers' Party mid-1950s **rear l to r:** ?, T. Thompson, F. Oliver, H. Close, B.Lamb, ?, ?, H. Davison **middle:** C. Leighton, Brad Laverick, T. Owen, Walter Laverick, S. Johnson, Alan Laverick, P.Hedley, ?, ?, Ernie Hope. **front:** E.Williams, J. Hird (manager), Tom Laverick, F. Bell, T. Oysten.*

*A gang of craftsmen with a big job to do, putting up an aerial flight tower **rear:** A.Scarr, P.Blyth, Fred Thompson, Trevor Hartnell, ?, **front:** Eric Campbell, Joe Reed, Harnett (Leeholme), Gordon Hunter, Alan Thompson, ?*

Tommy Bradley, horsekeeper at Chilton, proudly showing off a trophy won at a local pony show 1950s

The opening of the pit head baths, Chilton 1949. First sod cut 8/7/48, first bricks laid 10/9/48. Some of the crowd: Brian Guy, Peter Davies, Billy Buckley, Brian Errington, John Steel. The boy is attempting to clean his boots on the rotating brushes.

Chilton Colliery Conclusion (a Personal Opinion)

A look at the mine plans showed Dean and Chapter coal reserves declining apace back in 1949, the coupling through to Leasingthorne, underground, increasing the tonnage up the shaft and probably doing little to bring about any sustained profitability. With Chilton swallowed up in all of this by 1960, the writing was on the wall. Coal production ceased in 1965, bringing to an end the village's association with mining going back 135 years.

By 1959 there would be little remaining in the way of reserves at Dean and Chapter or Leasingthorne compared to the huge amount in Chilton's southern reserves (which are still there), the Harvey and Hutton only partially extracted, and the Busty seam untouched.

One estimate was that Chilton Colly could well have worked a further 30 years at 9000 tons per week had the pit stayed in isolation from the other two. For that to happen, the old enemies, the water level and the market forces, were two factors among others which would need to stay in the pit's favour.

However, the reality is that the pit did not stay on its own and, as a consequence, our mining era was consigned to history sooner than it might have been.

Chilton Banner of about 1954.
standing l to r: *? ,?, Mrs. Gowland, Jim Taylor, Bill Williamson, ?, Mrs.Oldham, Hannah Parker, Sam Keenan, ?, Sid Slater, John Bolton, Ron Smith, Jim Mathews, Sid Shellborn, ?, Joby Read, Jack Ball, Tucker Williams, Andrew Kennedy, Ken Nattrass, ?, ?, Harold Allacker, John Daykin, Jimmy Keenan.*
sitting rear l to r: *Jim Mathews (jnr.) Ted Attwood, Twi Mason* **sitting l to r:** *George Clennel, ?, Tommy George, ?, Dick McKenna, Jimmy McKenna, Harold Allacker, George Metcalfe.*

CHAPTER TEN

Places of Worship

Places of Worship

Before the collieries, there were few buildings, no schools or places of worship, and only a handful of inhabitants occupying the houses forming The Square around three sides of the most important building at that time, a stagecoach stop, The Duke of Cleveland public house, as it was named from 1832 until 1902. These folk were in the Ferryhill Parish and more than likely, walked or used a horse and cart to attend a church or chapel at Ferryhill.

The Methodist Church

The first in Chilton was a tin chapel used by the United Methodists, to the rear of West Chilton Terrace close to the top of Dene Terrace around 1900. Mr Bill Hedley, lay preacher, ran this chapel. The Army took it over in 1939 and it never reopened. This was followed by the Lane Ends Primitive Methodist Chapel, erected in 1906. Although built as chapels with differing denominations, it appears they were amalgamated in 1932 and became Methodist Churches.

Chilton Lane Ends Primitive Methodist Church in 1991

Inside the Primitive Methodist Church, Chilton

*Regulars of the congregation **l to r:*** *Chris Hedley, Evelyn Bullman, Violet and Eric MacDonald.*

standing l to r: *Billy Hunter, John Nixon, Billy Welch, Jenny Croft, Mr. Hinson (minister), Mrs. Welch, Mrs. Hinson, Evelyn Bullman, Billy Jackson, Chris Hedley, Mrs. Jackson (organist).* ***sitting:*** *Freda Morrow, Lottie Henderson, Mrs.Farrow, Mrs.Patterson and Chris's grandson Joe Myers.*

Regretfully, this church closed in 1991 and the congregation said goodbye in style with a fish and chip party

In Windlestone, the Wesleyan Methodists erected a tin chapel some time after South View was completed, about 1890's. It closed when the Trustees purchased the land to the rear of New South View and built a new chapel, now a church. It opened in November 1913 and is still used to this day.

St. John's Ambulance, Chilton Quadrilateral Division, serving two purposes: its own functions and preserving a little of our heritage, a memory of the Salvation Army.

Windlestone Methodist Church facing west onto the main road through Chilton.

The Salvation Army

St. John's Ambulance concrete block building surrounds and protects the original hut/hall used by the Salvation Army Corps in Chilton. They had a Sunday School and their own band, a common sight around the streets, especially at Christmas and on anniversaries until its closure in 1940.

Walter Wade and his family, as residents of South View were typical of many, like families in our community. He was an envoy, a position similar to that of a lay preacher. Coloured lantern slideshows were popular with the children in the hall before World War II, but with the commencement of hostilities, the place was turned into a forces canteen, run by the Salvation Army. Walter Wade was also a keen member of St. John's in those days, rising to a Divisional Superintendent. It was providence that he was in an ideal position to purchase the hall for St. John's when the opportunity arose.

*This handbill makes a nice
reminder of a special day for many
of our residents.*

The Sacred Heart Church to the right adjoined by the Social Club on the left

The Catholic Church titled The Sacred Heart

Quite a big building overall, the church occupies the main hall of what used to be Windlestone Colliery Institute, the remainder of the building being given over to a popular social club run by the church.

Opened over 50 years ago on 11th April 1948, not only does it provide a spiritual and social need for the village, but in doing so it also is preserving a part of our heritage.

*Opening Day for the Sacred
Heart Church with a crowd of
churchgoers streaming through
the gates for the first service,
with some faces remembered
even to this day.*

St. Aidan's, Chilton Parish

Pre-1930.

Divine services were conducted in an end-of-terrace house in South View, Windlestone, on 25th November 1900. Through the generosity of the Rev. T. L. Lomax, who at that time was the vicar of Ferryhill Parish, St. Luke's of which St. Aidan's was a mission church, a church and hall were erected, of corrugated iron construction, on 11th July 1904.

The hall was used for Sunday School, social activities and meetings. It housed a billiard table, table tennis as well as other recreational games, with dances held on occasions.

The Mothers' Union was an active group, its members participating in pageants, working parties in sewing, knitting, rug making, sales of work and garden parties. Male members of the congregation organised football and cricket teams, with home and away fixtures.

To the south side of the hall was a boiler house and store, where the headmaster of the school next-door housed his car during term-time. On the north side, access was gained through a wicket gate in the hawthorn hedge separating the church and hall from the road. A wooden seat was placed there on which children and the aged could sit and admire the small flower beds.

The services were conducted by curates from St. Luke's. Mr. Redfern appears to have been a popular choice. Church Army Captains were also helpers. Sadly, this church was destroyed by fire on 12th March 1928. The damage was estimated at £4,000, the value of the fittings saved amounting to £80. Items rescued from the fire and still in use in the present church are brass candle-holders, brass vases, Bishop's chairs and robes. The altar frontals, banners and Communion vessels were also rescued.

The cutting of the first sod for the new church was performed on the north side by the Rev. T. L. Lomax and dedication of the site by the Venerable A. J. Rawlinson, DD, Archdeacon of Auckland on 27th April 1929.

Top: The aftermath of the fire: a pile of twisted tin sheets is all that remains of the Mission Church of St. Aidan's, 12th March 1928.

Bottom: Laying the first stone of the new St. Aidan's Church 1929.

Inside St. Aidan's

Consecration of the new St.Aidan's was on 10th May 1930 by the Rt. Rev. H. H. Henson, DD, Lord Bishop of Durham, in the company of a guard of honour formed by the Boy Scouts.

The new Church Hall, completed in 1928, was used for services until the church was completed.

St. Aidan's Church 1999

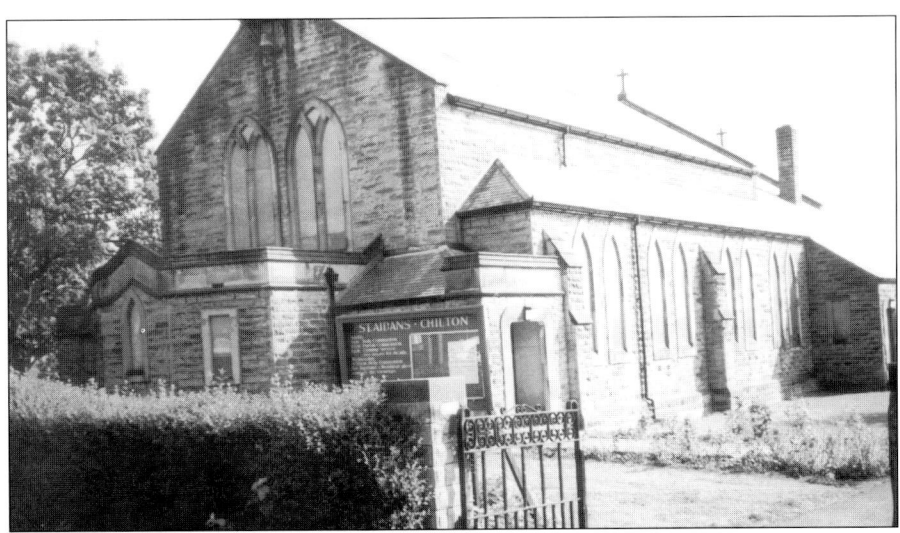

CHAPTER ELEVEN

To the Millennium

Chilton St. John's Ambulance Brigade

Chilton Division of the St. John's Ambulance Brigade was formed in 1928, Mr. John Croft of 20 Dene Bridge Row being the first officer. Their meetings were held in the "White House", probably the former mine offices in Windlestone Colliery pit yard. At this time the Brigade was sponsored by Chilton Colliery, Windlestone having closed four years earlier. There were about twenty members, the divisional surgeon being Dr. Mathew Hunter.

During 1934 an Ambulance First Aid Post was opened at Rushyford, which had become an accident blackspot with the increase in road traffic.

Dr. Mathew Hunter was a slightly-built man, no taller than 5 feet 2 inches. Always, a brown suit and trilby hat, and hardly ever without a cigarette in his mouth, either in his surgery or when visiting the sick. The surgery, a single storey building located to the rear of Hutton House, where he lived, is still there. He served the community for many years, attending accidents at the pit, and anywhere else for that matter, when called on to do so. On a sporting theme, he was a vice president of West Chilton AFC as far back as 1914 and a patron of Chilton RA in the 1920s.

His little two-seater Austin Seven with a fold-down hood was a common sight on his rounds. His ministrations helped many over more than 30 years of tending the sick. A man of the community, not surprising then to be asked to open the Regal Cinema in 1936. He became a village institution in his own lifetime and died in February 1948.

Founder members of the Brigade in Windlestone pit yard with the White House in the background.
2nd l: *Walter Wade, John Croft, ?, Dr. Mathew Hunter, ? (shown in greater detail on page 174)*

The full complement of the Brigade at Windlestone (shown in greater detail on page 174)

The opening of the First Aid Station at Rushyford 1934 by a senior brigade member. Looking on are probably two local dignitaries. ***First on the right:*** *Dr. Hunter, next to him John Croft.*

The First Aid Post

Founder members of the Brigade in Windlestone pit yard above with the White House in the background. ***2nd l:*** *Walter Wade, John Croft, ?, Dr. Mathew Hunter, ?*

The full complement of the Brigade at Windlestone about 1930

In the mid-1940s, the headquarters of the Brigade moved to the Social Centre (rear New South View), which previously had been in use as a British Restaurant. For many years before and after this time, the centre served the community for all manner of functions. Latterly until it was burned down in the 1970s, it was known as the Labour Hut.

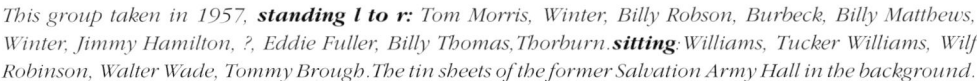

This group taken in 1957, **standing l to r:** *Tom Morris, Winter, Billy Robson, Burbeck, Billy Matthews, Winter, Jimmy Hamilton, ?, Eddie Fuller, Billy Thomas, Thorburn.* **sitting:** *Williams, Tucker Williams, Wilf Robinson, Walter Wade, Tommy Brough. The tin sheets of the former Salvation Army Hall in the background.*

By the mid-1960s this Brigade had the name Quadrilateral added to its title. A successful experiment involving regular weekly attendance and training for men, women, boys and girls being responsible. These four groups making it a Quadrilateral Division and this initial training was the spur that sent a number on to become nurses and army medical staff.

A more up-to-date group, probably late 1970s showing a mixture of members of all ages. Some are known l to r: Sandy Matthews, Colin Robson, Dick MacKenna (councillor), Lynne Jones, ?, Doug Newby, Marion Greathead, ?, ?, Dr. Spencer, ?, ?, ?, Tom Morris, Joe Ward, ?, ?, ?, Joe Leet (chairman of Sedgefield Borough), ?

The Brigade has attended many functions and gatherings, there, if needed, in case of accident or emergency. Some that spring to mind are Sedgefield Racecourse, football matches, carnivals throughout the area, gymkhanas and, not least, the accident which can happen anytime, anyplace, all done on a voluntary basis.

There is a long line of dedicated people who have been in the Chilton Brigade, a list far too long for these pages. Some have already been mentioned, others with 30 to 50 years' service, and one man, Tommy Morris, had 61 years of service, a record. Sadly he died in 1989.

A proud moment for Doug Newby of Chilton being presented with the highest award of Serving Brother and being made Captain at the same time, by Sir Miles Norman, standing in for the Duke of Gloucester on 13th May 1981.

The Brigade would not have existed without the unstinting support of all members of the community, whether it be the individual or the groups such as the churches, clubs, pubs,shops and businesses, for which I am sure the Brigade is most grateful. Alan Campbell now leads the Brigade,carrying on a tradition of service to the public, accepted and respected by all. Our sentiment should be,long may the St. John's Ambulance Brigade continue to serve and flourish into the next millennium.

Gone but not Forgotten

The Durham Miners' Gala has been in existence nearly 130 years. In those far-off days during the 19th century, it would have been hard to imagine a Gala Day without its collieries. Sadly, in 1994 this happened, with the closure of Easington and Vane Tempest, the last two British Coal pits operating in the once great Durham Coalfield.

The Gala still survives through the resolve of many redundant miners, their comrades from long-closed pits and the Union's leaders who continue to find financial backing to stage this great traditional event. Many of the banners still survive and are lovingly cared for, none more so than our own Chilton Banner. George Elliot, among others, has formed a committee whose aim is to look after the banner and raise the money needed to take it and a band to the Gala each year.

At this great event, three Union Lodges are invited to take their banner accompanied by their band to a Festival Service held in Durham Cathedral. For example, on 20th of July 1963 it was the turn of Crookhall, Washington "F" and Brancepeth Collieries to be asked. Even now, as it always has been, it is a moving experience. On this occasion in these magnificent surroundings the minister began by saying,

"Beloved, we have come here from the towns and villages of County Durham to this great Church, to worship God, to give thanks to Him for all His goodness to us, and to ask His help that we may serve him more faithfully in the time to come."

Towards the end of the service "The Voluntary" was played by Crookhall Band and a collection was taken at this time for the Aged Miners' Homes.

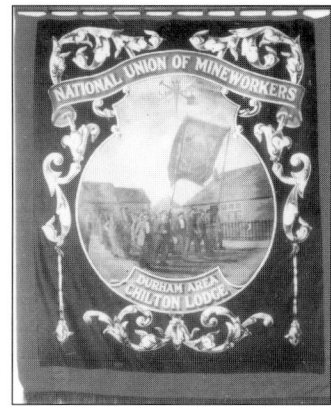

The reverse side of Chilton banner.

In all the years of this festival service Chilton has not once appeared, so it will be with great pride and a wonderful sense of achievement, when Chilton takes its place in the Cathedral on Durham Day in the year 2000 AD

The banner at the Centenary Miners' Gala 1983. **l to r:** *Dick MacKenna (Councillor), Jimmy Taylor, Sam Carmedy (Councillor), Peter Davies, Billy Hutchfield, Joe Leet (Councillor) Ginger Salisbury, Eric Campbell, George Porter (Councillor), Brian Swallwell.*

The lamp cabin where miners collected their cap lamps before going underground. One could be forgiven,looking at the condition outwardly, for thinking the pit was still working.

Above: The first colliery offices used by Henry Stobart & Co on the Dene Bridge site are to the right, taken 1905/6.

Below: The same offices, extended almost out of recognition to its present size as the pit expanded over its lifetime, and kept in excellent order by the present owners, Metal Drum Company.

A Coincidence.

Christopher Mason of Great Chilton Hall sank a pit shaft at Dene Bridge almost 160 years ago. It is a coincidence that the owners of the Metal Drum Company who now occupy this same site happen to live in Chilton Hall.

The Girl Guides and Brownies of 1972

There are many happy young faces here: some are named, the remainder I leave for the reader to puzzle over who's who.

Guides.
back row,2nd left: *Karen Turner, Marion Greathead, Denise Flook, Clare Dunn,*
Angela Rothery, Wendy Wilson.
2nd row: *, ?, Joanne Cairns, Liz Adams, ?, ?, ?,*
The Brownies.
Vicky Humphries, Jill Dunn, Caroline Denham, Joanne Greathead.

Community Force Centre

The centre is purpose-built to become the central communications facility for the Sedgefield Branch.

The new Community Force Centre, futuristic in design, both inside and out.

Community Safety Department

Eric Anderson is responsible for the day-to-day running of this department. It houses one of the biggest live Closed Circuit Television (CTTV) monitoring stations in the North of England.

The CCTV surveillance console keeps a 24-hour watch on more than 40 different locations across the borough.

These locations include several towns, such as Spennymoor, Ferryhill, Newton Aycliffe and Shildon.

A number of villages and some vulnerable locations are also monitored, Chilton main street is one of them.

Chilton Parish Council has purchased and installed CCTV to monitor the Welfare Grounds. The operation and maintenance of the system is carried out by the Community Safety Department giving a good example of partnership between the Parish and the Borough.

This centre is in the forefront, developing procedures for Control centres, In the future, National Training Courses will be developed and run from here.

Carelink

Carelink was formed in 1989 to care for the elderly residents on a 24-hour basis, 365 days each year, responding to calls within one minute. Arthur Bellwood is the Carelink manager.

The Carelink monitors make up part of the overall console, adjoining those of the Safety Department.

Carelink offers the very best of care for 7,000 elderly and vulnerable residents, all connected to the above control centre.

Rosewood Grange situated to the rear of the former Infant School in Chilton, is typical of the sheltered housing offered by Sedgefield Borough.

The resident warden is Doreen Smith, and the site warden Susan Gardiner; they respond to those in the community living in the bungalows.

*Top: Rosewood Grange
Bottom: A coffee morning in Rosewood Grange in aid of The Bishop Auckland Hospice in 1996. First lady on the left is Violet Cornish, then Walter and Mary Storey. The lady second right is Freda Morrow*

The Carelink monitors console which adjoins the Safety Department

Heading in the Right Direction

There is plenty of evidence of the changing face of the village in the past 35 years since the colliery closed. Some may have thought, this is the end, but as events have shown, the community at large has benefited from many improvements to its environment including housing, leisure and the workplace.

We still have some of the old places, others have made way for new ventures all in the name of progress, something that has been going on in Chilton, Windlestone and Rushyford for hundreds of years. The following photographs will bear testimony to this. Even so, there is no time for resting on our laurels: there is always something to do, something to make better.

Top: *Rookery Gardens, Rushyford*

Middle: *Large detached houses near the Eden Arms*

Bottom: *Mill Cottages: Old World charm*

Top: *Rushyford Cottages*

Middle: *Windlestone Farm House*

Bottom: *Rushyford Nursery, an attractive addition to the former Eden Estate Cottages*

Top: *These shrubs and bushes are planted the whole length of what used to be South View*

Bottom: *Vine Place , a smart, attractive car sales business, formally Oates Garage*

Top: I call this the precious
gems estate - diamond,
opal, jade etc. Built by the
council for miners working
at Chilton 1940s/50s, many
of these houses are now
privately owned. A very
pleasant, spacious estate.

Bottom: Eden Park Estate,
built by Wimpey on the east
side of Chilton

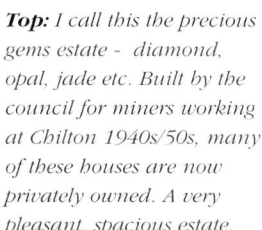

Whatever the Future May Bring

We are privileged to be here at such a momentous time in history. For many, the moment will not be lost, adults and children alike marking the occasion in some special way.

In the relatively short time span of our industrial and social history here in Chilton, there have been times when the resolve of our predecessors has been at a very low ebb, and for good reason. Strangely enough, the tide has turned at some point or other for the better and the community has soldiered on.

As the new millennium approaches, when one looks back, most of the problems of the past, given time, have been overcome. With this in mind, the community should have no fear of the future, only confidence in the ability to succeed.

Our hopes and expectations for the future rest on the shoulders of the children today. Here are some of them from the nineties and the coming millennium.

Happy, smiling faces, brimful of youth and vitality, and probably the best way to end our story.

Brian Turner, December 1999.

Class of 1991 **back row l - r :** *Ann Siddle, Kirk Truen, Clare Owen, Stuart Hubbard, Kelly Scott, Peter Hammond, Suzanne Day, Dean Robson, Leslie Jones* **middle row l - r :** *Peter Mathews (Head), Helen Bowles, Chris Flatman, Melanie Warwick, John Wallhead, Joanne Miller, Noel Duffy, Leanne Christie, Mark Turner, Tabitha Pattison, Mr. Ablett (teacher)* **front row:** *Brian Hughes, Kay Bunce, Chris Banks, Lisa Jay, Darren Maddison, Joanne Falls, Graham Stoker*

Class of 1992
back row l - r : *Steven Clark, Natalie McMullen, Andrew Tuesday, Tracy Hoot, Andrew Hughes*
middle row l - r : *Lee Thistlethwaite, Jane Wayman, ?, Lisa Gordon, Gary, ?, Darren Asquith, Sarah Fothergill*
front row l - r : *David Watson, ?, ?, Susan Dagga, Craig Howe, ?, ?,*

Class of 1994 **back row l - r :** *Brett Williams, David Bellwood, Jane Parker, Lisa Coulthard, Paul Wilkinson, Carl Smailes, Alex Amitozie, Donna Smith, Leanne Wright, Emma Ruffle* **2nd rear l - r :** *Emma Britan, Paul Hackworth, Jamie Bennet, Andrew Dixon, Michael Marshall, ?, Lee Jordan, Lori Beatie, Michael Cook, Michael Falls, Thomas Cook, Melissa Shaw, Danny Hooper* **3rd rear l - r :** *Kenny Ashton, Alex Middleton, Carly Philips, Sarah Johns, Tony Henderson, Dereck Kippling, Michael Bowtell, Johnathan Dunn, Neil Thompson, Shaun Goodchild, Nichola Hunter, Nichola Craddock* **front row l - r :** *Ian Ferry, Stephanie Hughes, Brian Jones, Mr. Ablett, Mrs. Hughes, Mr. Wallace, Miss. Dufton, Becky Rood, Andrew Layhaw, Helen Skinner, Simon Pendleton*

Class of 1999

back row l - r : *Philip Owens, Rebecca Smart, Liam Hall, Andrew Quincey* **2nd rear row l - r:** *Dave Wallace (Head), Michelle Thompson, Stephanie Tilley, Claire Cooke, Maisie Bamforth, Samantha Cooke, Jane Richardson (Teacher)* **3rd rear row l - r :** *Sarah Moody, James Bielor, Leanne Blench, Sarah Britton* **front row l - r :** *Sophie Craggs, Gareth Brown, Lauren Sayers*

This logo seen throughout the book was designed by Lucy Johns who won a competition at Chilton Junior School to design a logo for the new millennium. She was a member of Mrs. Jane Richardson's Year 4 class of 1997. A very good effort, well done Lucy!

Acknowledgements

I am especially grateful to Dave Wallace (headmaster), Chilton Junior School, for his help and enthusiasm.

There are a great number of people without whose support I would not have been able to complete this book: a little advice, a snippet of information and photographs - the list is endless. For those whose names who do not appear here, please accept my thanks.

Norman Turner	Mining information and photographs
John Thompson	His grandfather John Herriotts
Dave Williams	Copy of the D.M.A. History by John Wilson
Tommy Buckle	His memorabilia
Kathleen Oates	Photographs, books and Amy Johnson
Charlie Wayman	Footballer
Billy Lamb	Cricket / Homeguard
Geoffrey Hill	Aviation Historian (Amy Johnson)
Fred Thompson	Amy Johnson
Billy Davison	Amy Johnson
Jonica Brittain	Chilton Hall
Margaret Sowerby	Nathan Parkin
John Newbould	Rushyford Nursery
R. N. Dunn	Social and economic history of Chilton
Keith Baily	Photographs / copies
Avis Smith	Digital enhancement
St. Aidan's	Church history / photographs
Chilton Parish Council	For their support
Sedgefield Borough	Eric Anderson, Community Force Centre
Arthur Bellwood	Carelink
J. Snowball & Son	Design and Print
Doug Newby	St. John's Ambulance
The Eden family	Anthony Eden's book 'Another World'
Ordnance Survey	Their permission for reproductions
Chilton Junior School	Photographs etc.
Susan Bolam	Chilton Library